The American Utopian Adventure

SERIES TWO

FROM FLORENCE TO UTOPIA

From Utopia to Florence

The Story of a Transcendentalist Community
in Northampton, Mass.
1830-1852

BY

ALICE EATON McBEE, 2ND

WITH NEW DOCUMENTARY APPENDICES

PORCUPINE PRESS

Philadelphia 1975

First edition 1947
(Northampton, Mass. : Smith College Studies in History, Volume
Volume XXXII, 1947)

$$HX$$
$$656$$
Reprinted with additions 1975 by $$N75$$
PORCUPINE PRESS, INC.
Philadelphia, Pennsylvania 19107 $$M3$$
$$1975$$

Library of Congress Cataloging in Publication Data
McBee, Alice Eaton.
    From Utopia to Florence.

    (The American utopian adventure : Series two)
    Reprint of the 1947 ed., published in Northampton,
Mass., which was issued as v. 32 of Smith College studies
in history and as no. 8 of Smith College Council of In-
dustrial Studies series; with new additions by the pub-
lisher.
    Originally presented as the author's thesis (M.A.),
Smith College.
    Bibliography: p.
    1. Northampton Association of Education and Indus-
try. 2. Florence, Mass. I. Title. II. Series:
Smith College studies in history ; v. 32. III. Series:
Smith College. Council of Industrial Studies. Study ;
no. 8.
HX656.N75M3 1975   335'.9'74423   74-31281
ISBN 0-87991-027-5

Manufactured in the United States of America

WHAT I FOUND AT THE NORTHAMPTON ASSOCIATION

Frederick Douglass

Of the great mental wave of reform that passed over New England fifty years ago and gave rise to the Florence, Brook Farm, and Hopedale Communities, others can tell you more and better than I. The religion of good will to man; of fervent desire and courageous determination to put aside the old and to venture boldly upon the new; to change and improve conditions of human existence; to liberate mankind from the bondage of time-worn custom; to curb and fix limits to individual selfishness; to diffuse wealth among the lowly; to banish poverty; to harmonize conflicting interests, and to promote the happiness of mankind generally, had at that time such a revival as, perhaps, New England had never seen before, and has certainly never seen since.

This high thought of the time took deep hold upon men and women, and led them to dare and do startling things in contradiction to the common sense of the period. Many who thought themselves reformers were not ready to embark in the wild, or what seemed to them wild, and fantastical measures of these radicals who, in their war against old forms and social arrangements, sometimes seemed to assume that whatever was new, was true, and that whatever was old, was erroneous. With them, the old way was the wrong way, and the new was the right, or at least had within it the promise of the right.

The period was one of faith, hope, and charity; of millenial foreshadowing. The air was full of isms--Grahamism, mesmerism, Fourierism, transcendentalism, communism, and abolitionism. Fresh from slavery at that time, and keenly alive to its horrors, my mind was mainly occupied with the last mentioned ism, and yet with a strong leaning towards communism as a remedy for all social ills. I found, too, that the men and women who were interested in the work of revolutionizing the whole system of civilization were also deeply interested in the emancipation of the slaves; and this was enough to insure my sympathy to these universal reformers.

Of the various attempts to give form and substance to the broad and beneficent ideas of the times, Florence and Hopedale seemed fullest of promise. For harmony, Hopedale had a decided advantage over Florence, in that its leaders were of one religious faith, while Florence was composed both of men and women of different denominations, and of no religious bias or profession. It was from the first a protest against sectism and bigotry and an assertion of the paramount importance of human brotherhood.

I visited Florence almost at its beginning, when it was in the rough; when all was Spartan-like simplicity. It struck me at once that the reformers had a tremendous task before them. I knew that many of them were people well-to-do in the world and I naturally wondered how they could content themselves to leave the smooth and pleasant paths of life to which they were accustomed, for the rough and thorny ways they were now compelled to tread. The site of the Community was decidedly unpromising. The soil was poor and had little or nothing upon it but stubby oaks and stunted pines. The most hopeful thing I saw there was a narrow stream meandering through an entangled valley of brush and brier, and a brick building which the communists had now converted into a dwelling and factory. The place and the people struck me as the most democratic I had ever met. It was a place to extinguish all aristocratic pretensions. There was no high, no low, no masters, no servants, no white, no black; I, however, felt myself in very high society. I met there

Samuel Hill, Seth Hunt, George Benson, Hall Judd, William Bassett, James Boyle, Giles B. Stebbins, Elisha Hammond, his wife, Miss Sophie Foorde, and a number of others, all people from the upper walks of life, and yet fraternizing with the humblest members of the association of which they formed a part.

My impressions of the Community are not only the impressions of a stranger, but those of a fugitive slave to whom at that time even Massachusetts opposed a harsh and repellent side. The cordial reception I met with at Florence, was, therefore, much enhanced by its contrast with many other places in that commonwealth. Here, at least, neither my color nor my condition was counted against me. I found here my old friend, David Ruggles, not only black but blind, and measurably helpless, but a man of sterling sense and worth. He had been caught up in New York City, rescued from destitution, brought here and kindly cared for. I speak of David Ruggles as my old friend. He was such to me only as he had been to others in the same plight. Before he was old and blind he had been a coworker with the venerable Quaker, Isaac T. Hooper, and had assisted me as well as many other fugitive slaves on the way from slavery to freedom. It was good to see that this man who had zealously assisted others was now receiving assistance from the benevolent men and women of this Community, and if a grateful heart in a recipient of benevolence is any compensation for such benevolence, the friends of David Ruggles were well compensated. His whole theme to me was gratitude to these noble people. For his blindness he was hydropathically treated in the Community. He himself became well versed in the water cure system, and was subsequently at the head of a water cure establishment at Florence. He acquired such sensitiveness of touch that he could, by feeling the patitent, easily locate the disease and was, therefore, very successful in treating his patients.

David Ruggles was not the only colored person who found refuge in this Community. I met here for the first time that strange compound of wit and wisdom, of wild enthusiasm and flint-like common sense, who seemed to feel it her duty to trip me up in my speeches and to ridicule my efforts to speak and act like a person of cultivation and refinement. I allude to Sojourner Truth. She was a genuine specimen of the uncultured negro. She seemed to please herself and others best when she put her ideas in the oddest forms. She was much respected at Florence, for she was honest, industrious, and amiable. Her quaint speeches easily gave her an audience, and she was one of the most useful members of the Community in its day of small things.

It is hardly possible to point to a greater contrast than is presented by Florence now, and what it was fifty years ago. Then it was a wilderness. Now it blossoms like the rose. Though the outward form has changed, the early spirit of the Community has survived. The noble character of its men and women, and the spirit of its teachers, are still found in that locality, and one cannot visit there without seeing that George Benson, Samuel Hill, Mr. and Mrs. Hammond, Sophia Foorde, William Bassett, and Giles B. Stebbins, and the rest of them, have not lived in vain.*

---

*Article taken from *The History of Florence, Massachusetts,* edited by Charles A. Sheffeld, Florence, Mass., published by editor, 1895.

Number VIII

of

The Smith College Council of
Industrial Studies Series

TABLE OF CONTENTS

Preface ix

Chapter   I. In the Beginning 1

Chapter II. Not Quite Utopia 14

Chapter III. Exit the Community 41

Chapter IV. Enter Florence 67

Appendix 74

Bibliography 75

ACKNOWLEDGEMENTS

This study was originally submitted as a thesis in partial fulfillment of the requirements for a degree of Master of Arts at Smith College. The writer wishes to express sincere gratitude to Professor Randolph C. Downes, director of this paper, both for suggesting the subject and for his invaluable help, criticisms and encouragement in every phase of its development. The staffs of the Smith College and Forbes libraries in Northampton have been most cooperative and Miss Margaret L. Johnson and Mrs. Hazel Damon have been especially generous in contributing their time and information. Thanks are due to Mr. Zoltan Haraszti, Keeper of Rare Books, at the Boston Public Library for permission to consult letters in the Garrison Collection; to Yale University library for permission to obtain a photostat copy of the sections of the *Macdonald Manuscript* dealing with the Northampton Association; and to Mr. Allyn B. Forbes, Director of the Massachusetts Historical Society; Mr. Clarence S. Brigham, Director of the American Antiquarian Society; Mr. Robert H. Haynes, Assistant Librarian of Harvard College Library; Mr. Newton F. McKeon, Director of the Converse Memorial Library at Amherst College; Mr. Joseph Harrison, Librarian of the Forbes Free Library in Northampton; and Mr. Charles R. Green, Librarian of the Jones Library in Amherst for their cooperation in making available pertinent material in the possession of their various institutions. Mrs. Thomas Shepherd of the Northampton Historical Association was most kind in aiding in the location of useful documents; and Mrs. Marion Mack Sheffeld, Mrs. W. D. Gray, Miss Caroline Walker, Mr. Wilfred H. Learned and Mr. William M. Sheffeld were of great assistance in tracing the Association's record books. Research was materially aided by the helpfulness of the staffs of the Northampton Hall of Records and the City Clerk's Office.

PREFACE

This record of the development of a New England town is essentially the story of the Northampton Association of Education and Industry. It concerns an experiment in socialistic living which flourished during the decade 1840-1850 which saw men seeking to ward off the chill of materialistic society by turning their backs upon it and avidly warming themselves at the fires of transcendentalism and Fourierism. Three other Communities in Massachusetts found their source in this same movement, and their names have a more familiar ring: Brook Farm which brings to mind George Ripley, Channing, Margaret Fuller, John Dwight, and a score of other Bostonian intellectuals; Fruitlands, the half mad, half pathetic venture of Lane and Bronson Alcott; and Hopedale which, under the guidance of Adin Ballou, sought to spread the gospel of Practical Christianity. They are all gone now. Brook Farm is an orphanage; Fruitlands forms part of a tourists' mecca; and Hopedale is a sleepy crossroads. Their memory has been kept alive primarily through the reflected glory of their satellites. The Northampton Association has achieved a different immortality. For from this middle-class group, with strong convictions but without particular talents or distinction, developed a thriving industrial town where the Association itself is all but forgotten but where its spirit of religious tolerance and racial brotherhood survives.

The original records—personal and documentary—of the other societies have been carefully preserved by those interested in the sociological aspect of the experiments as well as those seeking biographical material about their famous members. Unfortunately this has not been so in the case of the Northampton Association. The Associationists themselves contributed in large part to their own obscurity, leaving behind them regretably few memorials either in writing or in legend, and their immediate descendants have been singularly careless of their fame. The official records of the Community consisted of a Journal, Letter Book, Secretary's Book and Account Book which were preserved until 1895. Then, after having been examined and discussed in part by Olive Rumsey in an article in the *New England Magazine* for that year, and more fully treated by Charles A. Sheffeld in his privately printed *History of Florence*, they disappeared. Every effort to rediscover them has proven fruitless and it seems almost certain that they, like so many historical documents before them, were classified as "rubbish cluttering up the attic" by some unthinking housewife, and vanished in the zeal of a New England housecleaning.

The members of the Northampton Association were for the most part industrious and hard working people concerned with the homely day-to-day tasks that had to be done. But in facing the stern realities of making a living they did not forget that they had banded together in an endeavor to create a better order of things, a more generous measure of freedom for all men, a higher and nobler conception of life based on the recognition of the intrinsic worth and dignity of the individual. So, in piecing together the story from newspaper and magazine articles of the period, real estate transactions, town records, letters, pamphlets, journals, memoirs and—when forced to do so by the absence of other authorities—from earlier chroniclers of the Association's history, every attempt has been made to evaluate the social and economic implications of the venture for the locality in which it flourished.

CHAPTER I

IN THE BEGINNING

American preoccupation with the problems of utopian socialism during the middle years of the nineteenth century manifested itself in a host of Communities, Phalansteries and Associations where men and women of almost every race, creed and color strove for a time together to create a perfect society. None of these communities existed in a vacuum. They were not set down here and there throughout the country completely at random; and when their period of productivity was at an end they did not vanish overnight, leaving no trace of their occupancy. Yet the trend has been to examine these products of an intellectual protest against the inequalities of the age solely as separate entities, almost, if not completely, divorced from the established communities in or near which they flourished. The influences which local situations exerted upon their formation, and the influences which they in turn exerted upon localities after experimentations with utopia crumbled before the stern demands of an uncompromising world, have passed almost unnoticed in the shadows while the spotlight has been focused upon the separate and several contributions which these Communities have made to the bulk of American social thought. The value of examining these phases of the history of the various Communities may, in some cases, be debatable, but in the case of the Northampton Association of Education and Industry there can be little question that the interaction of the economic life of the locality upon the Association and of the Association upon that of the locality was so great that a comprehensive discussion of the Association must perforce include these elements.

The destiny of the Northampton Association of Education and Industry was to no small extent influenced by a resident of Northampton whose name cannot be found among the lists of its members, patrons, or adversaries; and who in fact was so busily engaged at the time of its prosperity in enterprises of his own in another country, that it is more than probable he never even knew of the experiment until long after it had passed out of existence. Samuel Whitmarsh's inadvertent contribution to the Association grew out of his realization of the monetary potentialities of the interest in silk culture which was gaining momentum throughout New England in the 1830's.

The history of sericulture in America had, until this period, been sporadic and unpretentious. Its inception here at the instigation of James I of England in 1609 was inauspicious, for despite legislation which made it mandatory for plantation owners in the Virginia colony to plant ten mulberry trees for every one hundred acres of land held from the Crown

1

under penalty of fine; and despite the fact that a handsome premium was offered for every pound of native silk, both interest and production lagged and in 1666 the acts were repealed.[1] Late in the century French Huguenots revived the culture in South Carolina, but interest was localized and fitful until after the Revolutionary period when various states interested in stimulating industry again offered bounties. The nation as a whole, however, paid scant attention to the industry until a Congressional Committee on Agriculture presented a report on sericulture to the Secretary of the Treasury, Richard Rush, together with the request that he have a manual prepared on the growth and manufacture of silk. Rush, in complying with this request, prepared a two hundred and twenty page illustrated document entitled "Letter from the Secretary of the Treasury" (but better known as "Rush's Letter")[2] which was published in an edition of some 6,000 copies in 1830, and was received with a great deal of interest throughout the country.[3] At the same time Congress authorized the publication, at government expense, of a series of "Essays on American Silk and the Best Means of Rendering It a Source of Individual and National Wealth" by John D'Homerque and Peter S. Duponceau,[4] of which *The National Intelligencer* said: "These Essays prove, conclusively, that this country is peculiarly adapted to the culture of silk . . . the cocoons spun by the silk-worm of the United States, are superior to those of Europe, in the quality, and in the quantity of Silk which they evolve."[5]

When Samuel Whitmarsh came to Northampton in the spring of 1830 there was very little evidence of interest in this branch of agriculture which was receiving so much attention from Congressional committees and national periodicals. However, according to local tradition, a certain Joseph Clark of Northampton, "Gentleman," had been instrumental in introducing the mulberry into Hampshire county in the 1770's and had carried on an extensive correspondence about silk culture with the secretary of an English Agricultural Society as early as 1794.[6] Sufficient activity in the field had persisted to produce five claimants for the premiums offered by the Hampshire, Franklin and Hampden Agricultural Society for "the most mulberry trees planted" when the awards were made at its annual Fair and Cattle Show in 1831.[7]

Just how Mr. Whitmarsh, a retired merchant who had amassed a considerable fortune in the "Dry goods and Gents' furnishings" business in New

---

[1] *The Encyclopedia Americana* (New York, 1944), Vol. 25, p. 2-3.
[2] Shichiro Matsui, *The History of the Silk Industry in the United States,* (New York, 1930), p. 16.
[3] *The Americana, Op. Cit.,* p. 3.
[4] *Register of Debates in Congress,* Vol. VI, Part II, p. 869.
[5] *The National Intelligencer,* quoted in *The Hampshire Gazette,* February 17, 1830.
[6] *The Northampton Courier,* June 14, 1837.
[7] *The Hampshire Gazette,* May 1, 1833.

York City as a rival of A. T. Stewart,[8] first became interested in silk culture is unknown. But some of the property which he bought shortly after coming to Northampton adjoined that of a Mr. Starkweather[9] who was at the time the town's leading sericulturist, and it is not illogical to suppose that Mr. Whitmarsh's attention may have been drawn to the industry by his neighbor's activities. In any event, he did not become an immediate convert to the business but devoted his time for several years to building a large residence in the Fort Hill district of town and enlarging his property holdings in that section[10] on the one hand, and taking an active part in local politics on the other.[11] While Whitmarsh was thus engaged in establishing a reputation as a valuable and upright[12] citizen, general agitation for a widening of the silk industry continued to spread.

In February of 1831 the Massachusetts Legislature, emulating its national counterpart, requested that a "Concise Manual containing information respecting the Mulberry Tree with directions for the culture of Silk" be printed at State expense, and distributed to every town in the State.[13] Some six hundred dollars was appropriated for the purpose and the manual was compiled by J. H. Cobb of Derby, Connecticut, and published by the direction of Governor Levi Lincoln.[14] By 1833 the Legislature was advocating a bounty of one dollar for every pound of raw silk reeled in the commonwealth, and one dollar for every one hundred mulberry trees planted. It was stated in the recommendation that:

A field is here opened for a species of industry which at present is scarcely available at all, but if slightly encouraged might greatly add to the general mass of productive employment and wealth.[15]

Silk culture also received stimulus from the disciples of home industry who felt, with Henry Clay, that the nation must be emancipated from its dependence upon foreign capitalists, and urged in the periodicals of the day that Americans raise silk to supply their own needs instead of allowing the "ten millions of dollars which we expend annually, in silk stuffs, (to) operate as so much bounty to foreign agriculturists."[16] The advocates of protectionism also took up the cry maintaining optimistically:

---

[8] *Ibid.*, April 27, 1875.

[9] *Northampton Registry of Deeds, Record Book*, Vol. 64, p. 230, 258-259, hereinafter referred to as *Hampshire County Record Book*.

[10] *Ibid.*, Vol. 66, p. 93; Vol. 64, p. 677-678; Vol. 70, p. 509-510.

[11] *The Hampshire Gazette*, March 19, 1832; March 20, 1833 record that Mr. Whitmarsh held the influential position of first selectman.

[12] Mr. Whitmarsh's first recorded act upon coming to Northampton was to purchase a pew in the 2nd Congregational Meeting House for $150, (*Hampshire County Record Book*, Vol. 64, p. 159) thereafter he was referred to in all legal documents as "Samuel Whitmarsh, Gentleman."

[13] *The Hampshire Gazette*, December 7, 1831.

[14] *Idem.*

[15] *The Northampton Courier*, February 20, 1833.

[16] *The National Intelligencer*, quoted in *The Hampshire Gazette*, February 17, 1830.

Our cotton goods now find their way to the Indies; our bricks are equal to any in the world; and with a little national protection we shall soon cease importing silk and have raw silk enough to spare for a profitable export.[17]

The voices of the New England farmer and manufacturer were added to the chorus in praise of silk when they saw in it a possible wedge to stem the tide of western emigration which was stripping whole communities of their inhabitants, and sending the cost of labor sky high. It was this latter suggestion which appealed to the Northampton leaders who read with trepidation the long lists of "Farms for Sale" in the local papers, and looked with stern disapproval upon the glittering accounts of western life and opportunity which appeared upon these same pages. *The Northampton Courier* of April 2, 1834 voiced its opinion when it carried the following editorial:

Silk, we are impressed with the belief, will at some remote day become the staple commodity of Northampton . . . and it might save the population of New England from emigration and death with fever and ague in the Western country. Will not our people, who now complain of hard times, awake to new sources of industry and do something which can be done to increase their pecuniary gains?

The ease and simplicity of silk culture were stressed and reference was made over and over again to its suitability as an occupation for children and "young females." Mulberry trees were common, and the sizable profits to be had from the business were repeatedly pointed out; although, in Northampton during the early years of its popularity, caution was unmistakably mixed with enthusiasm. *The Hampshire Gazette* pointed out:

Mr. Starkweather, of this town, sold his raw silk the present season at $4.00 per pound, but thinks he might have obtained $4.50. He says so much of the work is performed by women and children, that producing raw silk at $4.00 or $4.50 may be considered fair business though not very lucrative.[18]

Nevertheless, the Hampshire, Franklin and Hampden Agricultural Society in its Annual Report for 1832 emphasized Northampton's suitability as a place for growing mulberries and evinced the hope that it would "ere long, become one of the most important staples of our country."[19] In the years 1833-34 a steadily increasing amount of space was given over to silk culture in both the advertising[20] and news sections of the *Gazette* and the *Courier*.

[17] *The Northampton Courier*, April 3, 1833.
[18] *The Hampshire Gazette*, October 31, 1832.
[19] *Ibid.*, November 14, 1832.
[20] Interestingly enough very few of these advertisements for mulberry trees and seed were ever paid for, if the "Day Books" of Sylvester Judd, Editor of the *Gazette* until 1834, may be adjudged correct.

It was not until April 22, 1835, however, that any indication of Mr. Whitmarsh's interest in silk found its way into the public press. On that date the following notice appeared in the *Hampshire Gazette* under the heading AFFAIRS OF NORTHAMPTON:

It may gratify some, to be informed what business operations are contemplated in Northampton the coming season. . . . Mr. Whitmarsh has embarked in the silk business on a great scale. He has now under cultivation thousands of Morus Multicaulis and is putting up a building two hundred feet in length, a part to be occupied with machinery for reeling and throwing silk, and a steam engine, and the remainder, by the reptile spinners. . . . Dr. Stebbins and Mr. William Clark, Jr. are also engaged in this business.

What may have seemed to the general public as a private business venture comparable to those of Messrs. Clark, Stebbins and Starkweather, albeit on a slightly larger scale, was in reality the beginning of a new era in Northampton's industrial life, the foundation upon which the Association of Education and Industry was to base its hopes of financial success, and, ultimately, one of the chief factors in the development of the present town of Florence.

Mr. Whitmarsh had, after studying the rudiments of silk culture and weighing the temper of the times, decided that there was a great future in the field of silk manufacture as well as that of silk culture. He therefore conceived of the idea of organizing a silk company in Northampton[21] which would raise and manufacture its own silk. Before taking active steps to locate outside capital, he set about purchasing suitable land for the undertaking. Obviously such a factor would require property with a dependable supply of water power for the operation of the machinery, and at the same time it would be necessary to be sufficiently close to an easily accessible supply of labor. These primary requirements seemed to be satisfactorily complied with by a group of farm lands and meadows lying about three miles west of the village along the Mill River in a district known variously as "Boughton's Meadows" and "The Warner School District."[22] The immediate area was thinly settled, (not more than seven or eight family names appear in the County Record Books) but workers could be easily hired in Northampton and the land, eminently suitable for mulberry plantations, was easily obtained. According to the *Hampshire County Record Books,* Ebenezer Hunt sold Samuel Whitmarsh and his brother Thomas Whitmarsh of Brooklyn, New York, twenty acres in "the Great Pastures, so called" on May 6, 1835 for $2,500.[23] William Clark "yeoman" received some $3,500 for an undesignated amount of

[21] L. P. Brockett, *The Silk Industry in America,* (1876), p. 55.
[22] Charles A. Sheffeld, *The History of Florence, Massachusetts,* (Florence, 1895), p. 57.
[23] *Hampshire County Record Book,* Vol. 76, p. 22. This is the only one of the transactions in which the name of Thomas Whitmarsh, who later became a member of the Northampton Association of Education and Industry, is mentioned.

meadow land, on June 4, 1835;[24] while Gaius and William Burt sold their holdings to the extent of one hundred acres "including their Home Farm . . . with part of its boundaries on the road to the oil mill" for $6,000 on September 11, 1835.[25] That same day Mr. Whitmarsh also purchased ninety acres from William W. Thompson and Eliza S., his wife, for $7,500.[26] This last named piece of property contained the oil and grist mills so frequently mentioned as boundaries or points of identification in the other deeds. Both of these mills had been operated by Josiah

[24] *Hampshire County Record Book*, Vol. 72, p. 338-339.
[25] *Ibid.*, Vol. 76, p. 164.
[26] *Ibid.*, Vol. 77, p. 158.

MAP OF FLORENCE 1831

Redrawn by C. L. Gethman from the original in
the Northampton Registry of Deeds.

White, Thompson's father-in-law, as late as 1828,[27] and were presumably, in good condition.

Once sufficient property had been secured, Mr. Whitmarsh turned his attention to enlisting the interest and financial support of others. He seems not to have approached his fellow townsmen, or at any rate, not to have succeeded in convincing them of the validity of his scheme, for no local names other than his own are to be found on the list of stock holders. Among his friends and former associates in New York City, however, he met with great success and by September 25, 1835 was able to dispose of all his recently acquired property for the sum of $40,000. In the deed Charles H. and Edward A. Russell, and Charles St. John are specified as Trustees of "An association of individuals formed for the purpose of carrying on the business of the culture and manufacturing of Silk. . . . The name to be The Northampton Silk Company."[28] No public notice of these transactions appeared until October 14th of that year (1835) when the *Hampshire Gazette* inserted this article in the "town news" column:

NORTHAMPTON SILK COMPANY—we are happy to be able to announce that Mr. S. Whitmarsh has purchased three hundred acres, mostly of interval land, about three miles west of this village, with an Excellent water privilege, an inexhaustible quarry of fine building stone, mills &. . . . which he conveys to a stock company formed for the purpose of cultivating and manufacturing Silk. An act of incorporation with capital adequate to an extensive prosecution of the business in all its branches, is to be applied for at the ensuing session of the Legislature. . . . Mr. Whitmarsh has sailed for Europe in order by personal observation to acquaint himself with the practical details of the contemplated business.

To this notice the *Northampton Courier* for October 21st added that the organization and commencement of the business would take place when Mr. Whitmarsh returned to Northampton in the Spring of 1836.

While the activities of the Northampton Silk Company were held in abeyance, silk culture in general was receiving greater stimulus through the medium of direct subsidies in almost all of the New England and some of the Southern states,[29] and through the introduction of the Morus Multicaulis, a variety of mulberry whose growth was more rapid, and whose foliage was larger and denser than that of other species. As the fame of this variety spread nurserymen began to get more demands than they could conveniently supply. The price of the Multicaulis in this country rose from $4.00 a hundred in 1834 to $10.00 in 1835, and by

[27] *Ibid.*, Vol. 60, p. 650-651.
[28] *Ibid.*, Vol. 72, p. 359-361.
[29] *U.S. Census of 1880, Report of the Silk Manufacture of the U.S.*, Vol. 2, p. 919-920, quoted in Matsui, *op. cit.*, p. 16.

the beginning of 1836 had reached an unprecedented high of $30.00 the hundred.[30] Mr. Whitmarsh wrote from France that his extensive purchase of the Multicaulis seed there on behalf of the Silk Company had resulted in raising the price abroad nearly fifty per cent.[31]

The financial boom in mulberries both at home and abroad removed most of the skepticism with which Northampton at large seems to have regarded Whitmarsh's ventures, and the *Courier* on February 24, 1836 reported with pride that Northampton stood at the head of places where the business of silk culture had been attempted. An editorial in this same issue stated:

> The plan of embarking on the Silk business will not be urged with extravagant enthusiasm beyond what facts and fair reasonings will justify, but such statements will be given and arguments used, as will convince our agricultural friends there is no necessity for New England men, emigrating to the West for lack of lucrative employment at home. . . .

The issue for March 30, 1836 reported:

> Sewing silk is selling in this town at $10½ per pound . . . already we feel the necessity of having our Northampton Silk Company in operation . . . not less than $15,000 worth of silk stuffs were sold in this town during the year 1835 . . . if our farmers had had the business of silk growing . . . this comfortable amount could just as well (have) been put in their own pockets.

In April, Mr. Whitmarsh returned to Northampton[32] having traveled at length through the silk districts of France, Italy and Lombardy observing all phases of silk culture and manufacture.[33] By May the trees which he had imported for the use of the Silk Company arrived as well as an additional supply (presumably purchased with his own funds for speculation purposes) which was offered to the public to $30 to $35 the hundred for trees three feet in height or over.[34] Shortly thereafter, the Northampton Silk Company, which had been formally incorporated by an act of the Legislature during the Spring,[35] began active operations under the guidance of its officers: Samuel Whitmarsh, President; Charles N. Talbot, Edward A. Russell, Christopher Hubbard, James Bowen, and S. Whitmarsh, Directors; Charles St. John, Treasurer; and William H. Schofield, Clerk.[36]

They proceeded to stock about a hundred acres of their three hundred acre enclosure with engrafted trees, at the same time preparing more

[30] *Matsui, op. cit.,* p. 17.
[31] *The Hampshire Gazette,* March 23, 1836.
[32] *Ibid.,* April 27, 1836.
[33] *Ibid.,* March 30, 1836.
[34] *The Hampshire Gazette,* May 11, 1836.
[35] Sheffeld, *op. cit.,* p. 57; also the *Hampshire Gazette,* April 27, 1836.
[36] *The Hamphire Gazette,* June 8, 1836.

ground with a view to expansion another year.[37] The old oil mill was pressed into service as a temporary factory, and the most modern machines for manufacturing silk, made by Nathan Rixford of Mansfield, Connecticut (a pioneer in the invention of improved machinery for silk winding, doubling and spinning) were installed[38] there pending the erection of a proper factory building which was scheduled for construction in the fall.[39] In June of 1836 the Company had things sufficiently under control to be enabled to insert their first advertisement in the local paper, in which they announced that they would pay cash for cocoons and raw silk delivered to their establishment at "the Oil Mill Place" and that their price would vary from $3.50 to $5.00 per bushel for the cocoons depending upon quality.[40]

Evidently the response to this advertisement was not sufficient to supply their needs for the Company was obliged to import raw silk[41] in order to get their machines into operation, although Mr. Whitmarsh predicted that by another year this cocoonery would be able to supply the wants of the factory and furnish raw silk to other customers as well.[42] This optimism as to the prospects of the Company seems to have been shared by Daniel Webster for after a three day visit to Northampton in July, 1836, he "expressed himself highly gratified with what he saw ... (and) ... he had the fullest confidence in their (The Northampton Silk Company's ultimate success."[43] Nevertheless, practical limitations forced the company to restrict its output to sewing silk and ribbons[44] for the first six months of operation.[45] During this period a Congressional committee had been expected to visit and examine the works of the Company, and great hopes were laid upon the beneficial effects which the favorable report of such a committee would have upon public confidence;[46] but there is no conclusive proof that this projected visit ever actually occurred.[47] The Company, nevertheless, forged ahead purchased some new property[48] and installed machinery for weaving plain and figured satins, samples of which, according to local tradition, were taken to Washington and presented to Henry Clay, Daniel Webster and A. A.

[37] *Ibid.*, May 18, 1836.
[38] Brockett, *op. cit.*, p. 53, 55.
[39] *The Hampshire Gazette*, May 18, 1836.
[40] *Ibid.*, June 15, 1836.
[41] *The Northampton Courier*, July 27, 1836.
[42] *Ibid.*, June 22, 1836.
[43] *Ibid.*, July 20, 1836.
[44] *The Hampshire Gazette*, August 3, 1836.
[45] The ribbons were manufactured on French steam-powered reels; (*Hampshire Gazette*, July 29, 1836).
[46] *The Hampshire Gazette*, August 17, 1836.
[47] Mr. Sheffield says in his *History of Florence* that this committee was made up of Daniel Webster, Abbott Lawrence and James K. Mills, but I have been unable to find any confirmation of his statement in a source.
[48] *Hampshire County Record Book*, Vol. 79, p. 270.

Lawrence[49] as tokens of appreciation for the interest and encouragement they had shown toward the venture.

The new year, 1837, found the Northampton Silk Company producing over sixty pounds of sewing silk a week[50] which they offered for sale by the pound through their local retail agents Stoddard and Lathrop. They were also wholesaling it at their factory.[51] This silk was widely used by the tailors of the town and "pronounced by them to be a very excellent article, superior to the majority of Italian silk."[52] In fact it proved to be of such good quality, and became so popular that even when the Company was able to produce at the rate of some two hundred dollars worth a day they were unable to satisfy the demand in the New York market,[53] and the *National Intelligencer* declared it to be "The most extensive and well regulated silk company in the Union."[54]

The financial panic of 1837 seems to have had very little visable effect upon the Northampton Silk Company other than a slight reduction in the number of employees.[55] This in no way affected their ability to provide "a full supply of Black and Blue Black and colored Sewing Silk put up neatly in half pound papers,"[56] nor did it limit their offer to supply "Merchants and Tailors at manufacturers prices."[57] The period of financial stress sowed the seeds of eventual ruin for the Company, however, because feverish attempts to recoup lost or dwindling fortunes added an impetus to the widespread speculation in mulberry trees, a speculation based only on a desire to get-rich-quick, and not upon any valid need for the trees. The Morus Multicaulis became in such demand that the top prices of 1836 appeared ridiculously low and it was by no means unusual for trees to sell one a week at twelve and a half cents apiece and be worth fifty cents to a dollar the next.[58] Such enormous profits encouraged dealers and nurserymen to expand their supplies and even to force trees in hot houses.[59] The amount of State bounties paid out to silk increased from $71.37 in 1836 to $350.52 in 1838[60] which in itself indicates the immense increase of activity in the field. Every available corner of the Silk Company property, including one hundred and twenty acres especially purchased for the purpose,[61] was stocked to overflowing with trees. Under ordinary

[49] Sheffeld, *op. cit.*, p. 59; also Brockett, *op. cit.*, p. 55.
[50] *The Northampton Courier*, January 11, 1837.
[51] *Ibid.*, January 13, 1837.
[52] *The Hampshire Gazette*, February 1, 1837.
[53] *Ibid.*, March 1, 1837.
[54] *The National Intelligencer*, quoted in the *Hampshire Gazette*, March 1, 1837.
[55] *The Hampshire Gazette*, May 31, 1837.
[56] *The Northampton Courier*, June 28, 1837.
[57] *Idem.*
[58] *The Hampshire Gazette*, September 12, 1838.
[59] *Ibid.*, January 16, 1839.
[60] *Ibid.*, April 3, 1839; see also *First Report of New England Silk Convention*, (Northampton, 1842), p. 19.
[61] Sheffeld, *op. cit.*, p. 60; also *Hampshire County Record Book*, Vol. 84, p. 382.

circumstances the losses of silk raising eclipsed the profits of silk manufacturing[62] and such rapid expansion put a severe strain upon the Company's resources. Only about $60,000 of the originally claimed $100,000 in capital stock had ever been raised,[63] and in the spring of 1838 they found themselves short of funds. The crisis was met by a stockholders' meeting where it was voted to subscribe an additional $30,000 immediately, and the Company was enabled to continue with renewed vigor.[64] But some retrenchment was necessary and on March 28, 1839 the County Record books reveal that the Capital stock of the Company "as fixed, limited and reduced from $100,000" stood at $94,450.[65] Their debts at this period amounted to some $42,494.18.[66] This financial excision was soon followed by a change in personnel. Mr. Whitmarsh and Thomas W. Shepherd, the company clerk and factory manager, withdrew[67] and Joseph C. Conant (one of the founders of the Mansfield, Connecticut Silk Company[68] who up until the time he came to Northampton had been associated with William Atwood and Harvey Crane in the manufacture of sewing silk and twist)[69] assumed the supervision of the factory. Conant brought with him Atwood and Crane's foreman,[70] Earle Dwight Swift, and another employee, Orwell S. Chaffee to assist him in the job of putting the factory on a profitable basis.[71]

Unfortunately for the company, the mulberry speculation bubble burst almost simultaneously with their efforts to reorganize. Prices dropped to pre 1835 levels overnight, and for a few weeks the market almost ceased to exist. An unusually cold and wet May had ruined many acres of the company's mulberry seed, and their acres of cuttings had fared almost as badly.[72] Faced with the necessity of importing raw silk in unexpectedly large quantities in addition to their other expenses, and with little or

[62] W. C. Wyckoff, *Report on Silk Manufacturing Industry of United States, Department of Interior, Census Office* (Washington, 1885), p. 16.
[63] Sheffeld, *op. cit.*, p. 60.
[64] *Idem.*
[65] *Hampshire County Record Book*, Vol. 84, p. 221.
[66] Sheffeld, *op. cit.*, p. 61.
[67] *Idem.*
[68] Brockett, *op. cit.*, p. 52.
[69] *Ibid.*, p. 57.
[70] *Idem.*
[71] Sheffeld, *op. cit.*, p. 61.
[72] *The Hampshire Gazette*, June 19, 1839.
——The exact reason for Mr. Whitmarsh's withdrawal is unknown but it may have been that the officers of the company, less enthusiastic about experimentation in sericulture and more interested in financial returns, felt that he was placing too much emphasis upon silk culture and too little upon silk manufacture. Needless to say, the fact that Mr. Whitmarsh, together with his brother Thomas, had been producing silk goods for sale at his own factory in the village since late in 1837 (cf. *The Hampshire Gazette*, November 22, 1837; June 13, 1838) did nothing to dispel these suspicions. It may also have been felt that Mr. Whitmarsh's other interests which included experimentation with Beet Sugar in Northampton, as well as his activities in such organizations as the United States Silk Society, of which he was vice-president, required him to spend too much time away from the problems of the Company.

no prospect of any reimbursement for the amounts spent on trees designed to meet the demand for Multicaulis, the stockholders became discouraged and set about liquidating the Company. The details of these operations are recorded in the Hampshire County Record Books, and it appears that the Company sold all their holdings to a body of the stockholders for $40,000 on May 20, 1839.[73] The first public announcement of the Company's decision to dissolve itself took the form of a "For Sale" advertisement inserted in the *Northampton Courier* of March 18, and the *Hampshire Gazette* for March 25, 1840. The advertisement gave full descriptions of the factory's location and equipment and then added: "The whole premises are well calculated for a Sugar Beet establishment, and worthy the attention of persons about to engage in that business. As the property will be sold within 30 days early application must be made." Evidentally no adequate bidder appeared for Charles N. Talbot, Henry H. Casey and Joseph W. Alsop, Jr., were appointed Trustees for the stockholders on June 19, 1840 with "power to manage, control, lease and let" or sell the property.[74]

During the transition period Joseph Conant continued to supervise the factory and produced seemingly satisfactory results even though operating on a reduced scale, as the comments of the Committee on Manufactures of the Hampshire, Franklin and Hamden Agricultural Society testified in their report to the *Hampshire Gazette* for March 17, 1841:

> The sewing silk, from the silk factory, made by Mr. Conant, was a good article. A piece of wide black ribbon attracted much attention. The silk hosiery and sewing and knitting thread were much admired.

Much of the Company's property lay uncultivated or was let out in small plots to local people for various purposes; about twenty acres were leased to Mr. David Child for experimentation with Sugar Beets, while the affairs of the Company remained in flux.[75]

In 1841 the Trustees once again advertised the property of the Silk Company for sale:

> MANUFACTORY, MACHINERY AND LAND FOR SALE. At Public Auction . . . known as the property of the Northampton Silk Company, will be offered for sale at the Mansion House of Col. Partridge, in the town of Northampton, on Thursday, the first day of April, 1841, at 12 o'clock noon. The factory is a splendid building of brick, with stone foundation, four stories high, built in 1837 of the best materials, with a valuable water power . . . on a never failing stream with sufficient water and fall for another manufactory of the same size. There is, also, on the premises, a saw and planing mill, and a wood factory of about 30 feet square. In the large building is machinery for the manufacture of

[73] *The Hampshire County Record Book*, Vol. 84, p. 380-383.
[74] *Ibid.*, Vol. 88, p. 301, 302-305.
[75] *The Hampshire Gazette*, July 1, 1840.

sewing silk to the extent of 150 pounds per week. . . . There are five framed dwelling houses for boarders and families, with a farm of 405 acres . . . on which are between 3 and 4,000,000 Alpine and other varieties of mulberry trees. . . . Its location is . . . where laborers are easily obtained, and the situation and climate exceedingly pleasant and healthy. . . .[76]

This advertisement was followed on April 14th by a notice in the *Gazette*.

The property of the Northampton Silk Company, in this town, was disposed of at auction, on the first day of April, for $22,250. . . . It cost the company, we understand, upwards of $100,000.

While this announcement terminated the life of the Northampton Silk Company, it heralded the beginning of the Norhampton Association of Education and Industry.

[76] *The Hampshire Gazette,* February 17, 1841.

CHAPTER II

NOT QUITE UTOPIA

Transition from silk company to socialistic community was gradual. The story of the ownership of the silk company estate between April 1, 1841, when it was supposedly sold at auction, and September 14 of that same year is not entirely clear from the records. The evidence revealed by documents filed in the Northampton Hall of Records does not coincide with the newspaper reports of the day. There is no legal record of any sale[1] of the property on April 1 to substantiate the *Hampshire Gazette* notice of April 14; and in view of the fact that the subsequent sale on September 14 was conducted by the Trustees of the Silk Company, it would seem safe to assume that the auction had failed to produce a satisfactory bidder, and the company, in order to prevent an even greater depreciation of the estate's value in the public mind, had bought in its own property. This apparently logical explanation of events is, however, somewhat shaken by the fact that the town's other newspaper, *The Northampton Courier*, carried a statement on May 26 to the effect that Mr. Joseph Conant, of Northampton, had purchased the "whole concern" of the Northampton Silk Company. Furthermore, a representative (unnamed) of the paper had recently visited the plant and found that Mr. Conant, having "full confidence in the business," had a "small part of the machinery in operation attended by about a dozen girls with male superintendents," and was also operating a shingle machine "which turns out shingles of a superior kind."[2] This report makes it appear that Mr. Conant was in possession of the property, especially since in all prior notices in both the *Gazette* and *Courier* he had been specifically referred to as "the agent of the Company." It is possible that some private arrangement had been made between Conant and the Trustees whereby he was to have control—nominally at least—of the property until such time as a sale could be arranged. As Conant was a member of the partnership which purchased the estate on September 14, it seems safe to assume that he may have been granted some such privilege while the negotiations for the formation of the partnership were under way.

At any rate, according to the *Hampshire County Record Books*, the Trustees of the Northampton Silk Company, Talbot, Casey and Alsop, upon receipt of $20,000 in cash transferred the Company's holdings, subject to the restrictions of prior deeds, to Joseph Conant of Northampton,

---

[1] There is no record of any prior sale to Conant in the *Hampshire County Record Books.*

[2] *Northampton Courier*, May 26, 1841.

George W. Benson and William Coe of Brooklyn, Connecticut, and Samuel L. Hill of Windham, Connecticut, on September 14, 1841.[3] The new owners almost immediately mortgaged the entire property, less forty rods which had been bargained to the Company's foreman, Earle Dwight Swift, to Charles N. Talbot (acting in this case as a private individual and not as a trustee for the Company) for $15,000;[4] thus obtaining a working capital sufficient to permit them to continue the business.

The circumstances which brought about the formation of the partnership of Conant, Benson, Coe and Hill can only be conjectured from the scanty information in existence. The fact that Mr. Conant's and Mr. Hill's wives were sisters[5] explains the relationship between these two men; and as the "For Sale" advertisements placed in the newspapers by the Northampton Silk Company had advised interested persons to "contact Mr. Conant on the premises,"[6] it is quite possible that Benson, who had just disposed of his family property in Brooklyn and was looking about for a place to settle.[7] may have become acquainted with Conant through placing an inquiry about the property. In any event, the three men had been in correspondence for some time befor the spring of 1841.[8]

The evidence of the extent to which this partnership was primarily based upon a desire to create a successful business enterprise is equally scanty, and in some cases contradictory.[9] Judging from Conant and Coe's subsequent actions, it may be concluded that they were more seriously interested in the original business venture than in the Association which developed from it; but as early as January, 1841, William Lloyd Garrison in a letter to Benson had made the following suggestions:

Where do you settle? . . . What say you to a little social community among ourselves? Brother Chace is ready for it, and I think we must be pretty bad folks if we cannot live together amicably within gun-shot of each other.[10]

It is quite probable, however, that George Benson needed no suggestion from his brother-in-law (Garrison had married Helen Eliza Benson on September 4, 1834)[11] or anyone else to turn his mind toward the Association

[3] *Hampshire County Record Book*, Vol. 92, p. 270-271.
[4] *Ibid.*, Vol. 93, p. 73.
[5] Sheffeld, *op. cit.*, p. 68. See also signatures in *Hampshire County Record Book*, Vol. 95, p. 231.
[6] *The Northampton Courier, op. cit.*, March 18, 1840; also *The Hampshire Gazette, op. cit.*, March 25, 1840.
[7] *William Lloyd Garrison, 1805-1879;* the story of his life told by his children (New York, 1885), Vol. 3, p. 25. Hereafter referred to as Garrison.
[8] Sheffeld, *op. cit.*, p. 68.
[9] Sheffeld maintains Mr. Hill was the originator of the Association while Olive Rumsey in "The Northampton Association of Education and Industry" in *New England Magazine*, New Series, Vol. 12, (1895), p. 23, states that Hill was primarily interested in the silk business.
[10] Garrison, *op. cit.*, Vol. 3, p. 25; letter was dated January 7, 1841.
[11] Garrison, *op. cit.*, Vol. 1, p. 427.

movement. He had been reared in an atmosphere of radicalism and reform, for his father, a retired merchant, who had been one of the founders of the Providence abolition society in 1790,[12] had sponsored Benjamin Lundy, The Quaker abolitionist and the first American to preach the gospel of negro liberty.[13] The elder Benson was also closely associated with religious reform and leaving the Baptist Church to become a Quaker he had enlisted his services in the cause of universal peace and at the time of his death was President of the Windham Peace Society.[14] George himself had become active in the anti-slavery cause at an early age, and William Lloyd Garrison, writing to Benson's brother Henry[15] in 1831, said:

I have had the pleasure of taking your brother by the hand and of holding an interesting tet a tet with him on the subject of slavery . . . he is, I am glad to find, sound in the faith. . . . Would to Heaven there were a host of such men enlisted in the glorious cause of universal emancipation.[16]

This interest led him to offer his services, together with Samuel J. May, in the defense of Miss Prudence Crandall when she was called to trial in March of 1833 for conducting a boarding school for colored girls in Canterbury, Connecticut,[17] and in May of 1834, the *Herald of Freedom* records his presence in New York City as a representative of the *Liberator* at the national meeting of the American Anti-Slavery Society together with Henry C. Wright.[18] Benson's activities and interests were not channelized in this field, however, as is attested to by the fact that Henry C. Wright requested him to "concoct a Declaration of Sentiments and Constitution, or a Constitution . . ."[19] and to fix upon a name for a universal peace society. According to the *Liberator,* Benson's document was accepted at an ensuing convention and he was elected to the Committee to nominate permanent members of the Society.[20] Another, and perhaps

[12] Constitution of a Society for Abolishing the Slave Trade; (Providence, 1789), quoted in Garrison, *op. cit.,* Vol. 1, p. 425.
[13] Excerpt from *The Life of B. Lundy,* p. 26; quoted in Garrison, *op. cit.,* Vol. 1, p. 87.
[14] Larnerd's *History of Windham County,* Vol. 2, p. 488-506; quoted in Garrison, *op. cit.,* Vol. 2, p. 120.
[15] Henry E. Benson became Secretary and General Agent for the Massachusetts Anti-Slavery Society in 1835 and held that post until his death in 1837. Annual Report Massachusetts Anti-Slavery Society, 1837, p. 71; quoted in Garrison, *op. cit.,* Vol. 2, p. 121-122.
[16] Letter to H. E. Benson dated August 29, 1831; quoted in Garrison, *op. cit.,* Vol. 1, p. 274.
[17] Letter from P. Crandall to W. L. Garrison, February 12, 1833; and letter from Arnold Buffum to Garrison, February 16, 1833; quoted in Garrison, *op. cit.,* Vol. 1, p. 317, 319-320.
[18] *The Herald of Freedom,* Vol. 6, p. 126; quoted in Garrison, *op. cit.,* Vol. 2, p. 355-356.
[19] Letter from Edmund Quincy to W. L. Garrison dated August 10, 1838; quoted in Garrison, *op. cit.,* Vol. 2, p. 224.
[20] *The Liberator,* Vol. 8, p. 155; Quoted in Garrison, *op. cit.,* Vol. 2, p. 224.

from the viewpoint of this discussion most important, interest of Mr. Benson's was in religious reform. He was present at the Charden Street Chapel in Groton, Massachusetts, for the three day meeting of the Rhode Island State Society in November of 1840[21] which had been called to consider universal reform of the church and to:

examine the validity of the views which generally prevail in this country as to the divine appointment of the first day of the week as the Christian Sabbath, and to inquire into the origin, nature and authority of the institutions of the Minister and the Church, as now existing.[22]

The topic under consideration had a widespread appeal for all those interested in the reform movement, and at this meeting Benson had an opportunity to listen to, and perhaps talk with, such men as George Ripley, William Henry Channing, and Theodore Parker who were so soon to be instrumental in the founding of the Brook Farm Association at West Roxbury.

Samuel L. Hill, the fourth member of the partnership, while not in a financial position[23] to devote his time to participation in these various reform societies, had many interests and aspirations in common with Mr. Benson. Mr. Hill had been reared in a liberal Quaker family in Rhode Island. After his marriage and removal to Willimantic, Connecticut, however, he joined the Baptist Church there and became one of its leading members until an anti-slavery meeting conducted by Wendell Phillips, which Hill had sponsored, was broken up by an angry mob of his fellow churchmen. This action estranged Mr. Hill from the Baptist sect and, after careful consideration, he formally withdrew from the society and remained unaffiliated with any specific religious sect for the rest of his life. In addition to his abolitionist sympathies, Mr. Hill was an ardent reader of the *Liberator* and was in touch with the theories and ideas of the Boston Transcendentalist movement,[24] as well as conversant with the variety of socialistic and cooperative idealisms which were prevalent at that time, when, as Emerson said, there was "not a reading man but . . . (had) . . . a draft of a new community in his waist-coat pocket."[25]

The compatibility of Mr. Benson's and Mr. Hill's views in regard to slavery, religion and the ills of the existing social system, undoubtedly soon led them to give serious consideration to the feasibility of starting a cooperative Association in Northampton, with the properties of their

[21] Garrison, *op. cit.*, Vol. 2, p. 422-425.
[22] *Idem.*
[23] Sheffeld, *op. cit.*, p. 206.
[24] All the biographical material dealing with Mr. Hill was derived from *The Hampshire Gazette, op. cit.*, April 21, 1866, April 2, 1867, December 19, 1882, and Sheffeld, *op. cit.*, p. 67-68; 205-208.
[25] Letter from Emerson to Carlyle quoted in Harry W. Laidler's *A History of Socialistic Thought* (New York, 1927), p. 123-124.

recently formed partnership as its industrial nucleus and economic mainstay. Before any public announcement of the projected scheme was made, they were joined by William Adam. Mr. Adam was a Scotchman who had served for a time as a Baptist missionary in India, and after being converted to Unitarianism through the efforts of a Hindoo scholar, Rommohun Roy,[26] had come to the United States to take up the position of Professor of Oriental Languages at Harvard College.[27] In 1840 he had served, together with Wendell Phillips, George Bradburn, Isaac Winslow, Harriet Martineau, W. L. Garrison and others as a delegate of the Massachusetts Anti-Slavery Society at the World Anti-Slavery Convention in London.[28] When the ladies of the American delegation were refused admission to the Conference on the grounds that women were not eligible as delegates, Mr. Adam had created quite a stir by declaring: "That if women had no right there, he had none; his credentials were from the same persons and the some society."[29] After being overruled in the meeting he had drawn up a formal protest against the exclusion of the women which, when signed by his delegation and presented to the Convention as a memorandum, was refused a place among its printed proceedings.[30] In addition to his professional duties and anti-slavery activities, Mr. Adam was an author and lecturer, having published *Correspondence Relative to an Unitarian Mission in Calcutta,* Boston, 1825; and *The Law and Custom of Slavery in British India,* Boston, 1840.[31] He came to Northampton in the latter capacity on January 11, 1842[32] and delivered a lecture on the China War in which "he exposed the . . . absurdity of denying to China as an independent nation the right of maintaining her own 'peculiar institutions' " and denied England's right to subjugate China to its personal and selfish wills and wishes.[33] The lecture, according to the Northampton *Courier,* expressed "the sentiments of a warm-hearted Christian Philanthropist" (sic) and was "clothed in the rich and beautiful language of a refined and classical scholar."[34] It is quite possible that Mr. Adam had learned of Mr. Benson's and Mr. Hill's wish

---

[26] Rumsey, *op. cit.,* p. 22.

[27] *Northampton Courier, op. cit.,* August 27, 1843; *The Hampshire Gazette,* August 29, 1843; Sheffeld, *op. cit.,* p. 67; Rumsey, *op. cit.,* p. 22. However, according to R. H. Haynes, Assistant Librarian at the Harvard College Library, the Harvard Archives do not contain any record of Mr. Adam's tenure there.

[28] *The Liberator,* Vol. 10, p. 55; quoted in Garrison, *op. cit.,* Vol. 2, p. 353.

[29] *Ibid.,* p. 118-119; quoted in *Ibid.,* p. 369.

[30] W. L. Garrison to his wife, letter of June 29, 1840; quoted Garrison, *op. cit.,* Vol. 2, p. 382.

[31] This information was obtained through the courtesy of Mr. Allyn B. Forbes, Director, Massachusetts Historical Society. Both these articles are on file in the Society's library in Boston.

[32] *The Northampton Courier,* January 4, 1842; January 11, 1842.

[33] *The Northampton Courier,* January 11, 1842.

[34] *Idem.*

to establish a socialistic community through William Lloyd Garrison, and he undoubtedly took advantage of this opportunity to look over the proposed site of the Association and to confer with Hill and Benson about the project.

Evidentally Mr. Adam was favorably impressed with what he saw for he joined the group, and at a meeting held on February 15, 1842 in Northampton he was elected treasurer, and Joseph Conant, president of a company formed by the founders as the first step toward formal organization of the Association.[35] At this same meeting Benson, Coe, Conant, Hill, and Adam drew up a Preliminary Circular which contained a brief basic statement of their reasons for establishing a cooperative community, together with a series of Articles which described in detail the plan of the proposed Association's financial organization and gave a less explicit delineation of its industrial and social organization.[36]

Arnold Brisbane's *The Social Destiny of Man* had been published in 1840 and undoubtedly most, if not all, of the Northampton Association's founders were familiar, at least through the medium of the public press, with this presentation of the doctrine of Francois Marie Charles Fourier, the French "apostle of social harmony," in which Fourier's plan for communal living with its emphasis upon the adaptation of society and environment to the individual; the conservation of effort and the elimination of waste, were developed in great detail.[37] They were also, no doubt, equally well acquainted with the dictates of the Transcendentalist philosophy which, in its American application embodied an expression of some of Fourier's ideals together with a more sweeping conception of social and religious reform. This philosophy was championed by such intellectual leaders as Channing, Parker, and George Ripley, and had even taken on a distinctly feminist note under the influence of Margaret Fuller. The Transcendentalists, however, did not press their demands for reform beyond the requirements of personal spiritual freedom, and their concern with the Association movement was primarily for the creation of an ideal environment for self culture.[38] In after years Mr. Hill, recalling the organization of the Northampton Association, remarked that it "owed its origin to Fourierism in a measure, but it was not based on any single system of philosophy."[39] It is evident, however, from the appearance of certain phraseology in the Preliminary Circular that at

---

[35] Sheffeld, *op. cit.*, p. 73.

[36] Quoted in *Ibid.*, p. 69-72.

[37] Arnold Brisbane, *The Social Destiny of Man*, (Philadelphia, 1840) *passim.*; also, *The Encyclopaedia of the Social Sciences*, (New York, 1931), Vol. 6, pp. 402-404.

[38] *The Encyclopaedia of the Social Sciences*, *op. cit.*, Vol. 15, p. 75-77.

[39] Letter from S. L. Hill to the *Hampshire Gazette*, dated February 2, 1867, published April 2, 1867; also S. L. Hill in an interview quoted in W. A. Hinds, *American Communities*, (Chicago, 1908), p. 276.

the outset, the minds of its authors were dominated by Transcendentalist idealisms and they stressed:

The duty of those who perceive the necessity of reform, to associate together upon principles . . . best calculated to fulfill the designs of God, . . . the progressive culture and high development of all the powers and faculties of our nature; the union of spiritual, intellectual and practical attainments; the equality of rights and rank for all, except that those stations and pursuits shall be regarded as most honorable which promote self-conquest and the most expansive philanthropy; and the practical recognition of the responsibility of every individual to God alone in all his pursuits.[40]

It was further stated:

Existing institutions . . . of business do not afford . . . the full development of the faculties of any class or individual; recognize invidious distinctions, . . . establish separate and conflicting action for various kinds and degrees of culture, skill and labor . . . separate labor from speculative pursuits so as to make it drudgery. . . .[41]

They seemed fully convinced that the associative principle would not only prove to be a panacea for this evil condition, but would ultimately revolutionize and indeed take the place of the competitive system in the economic world.[42] In forming this Community they believed that they were merely anticipating the general reform, and, in reality, hastening its accomplishment. This is a fact which helps to explain why Conant and Coe, who were hard headed business men with a wealth of practical experience behind them, could subscribe to the tenets of the new order.

The Association hoped to create a "better state of society" based on a dualistic control of capital and labor, or as the Preliminary Circular termed it: "The management of the affairs and undertakings . . . shall be conducted by two distinct companies . . . a Stock Company (and) an Industrial Community."[43] In order that the experiment might begin its operation on a sound economic basis, provisions were made for the Stock Company to be formed before the Industrial Community came into existence. Article III of the Circular stipulated that a subscription of $100,000 was to be solicited. If, however, $50,000 had been obtained by binding subsciptions and at least $30,000 of this paid in by April 1, 1842, the Association was to be organized; a president, secretary and treasurer were to be chosen to serve as trustees, and they, together with duly appointed stock directors, were to select twenty families to "commence the Industrial Association."

[40] Preamble to Preliminary Circular.
[41] *Idem.*
[42] S. L. Hill in an interview quoted in Hinds, *op. cit.*, p. 279.
[43] Article II.

All the financial concerns of the Community were to be administered by the trustees, who, however, were explicitly enjoined, in Article IV, to refrain from buying or selling as agents of the company on credit. The stock directors were empowered to determine the manner in which funds were to be invested and to make appropriations for carrying out the different branches of business within the Association.[44] The purchase of a share of stock entitled the subscriber to membership in the Stock Company. These stocks sold at $100 the share, were negotiable, when endorsed by both the president and secretary, carried an annual interest "not exceeding six percent," which was "not payable under four years."[45] Cash payment of interest or dividends accruing from the stock could not be demanded unless "notice be given to the Secretary thirty days before the payment becomes due."[46] In theory, persons (usually well-wishers and interested but unconverted sympathizers) who were not members of the Industrial Community could become stockholders, but Article XIII of the Circular explicitly stated that every share of stock was to contain a provision to the effect that "the shares owned by persons not members of the Industrial Association may be bought in upon payment of principal and interest by members of the Association," if notice was given thirty days before such time as the annual interest became due. In stock transactions every share was to be entitled to one vote, but a limit of ten votes per stockholder was to be enforced. Absentees could vote by proxy if they wished.[47]

The scheme by which labor was to be raised from the drudgery that in the outside world caused it to be "the degradation of a necessary means of education, health and happiness"[48] was primarily drawn from Fourier's plan of associative labor."[49] Every branch of employment was to be classed as a Division.[50] and was to operate under the supervision of a board of directors chosen by the stock trustees.[51] In accordance with Fouriers suggestion for making labor attractive[52] the members of the Association were to be free to select which branch of labor, or division, they wished to work in, and the members of each division were to choose their own leader to keep account of the work and skill of every individual and to report the progress of the group to the board of directors "annually and as often as necessary."[53]

[44] Article XV.
[45] Article IX.
[46] Article X.
[47] Article XII.
[48] Preamble to the Preliminary Circular.
[49] Charles Gide, Ed. *Selections from the Works of Fourier,* (London, 1901), passim.; hereinafter referred to as Fourier.
[50] Article XIX.
[51] Article XVIII.
[52] Fourier, *op. cit.,* p. 163-170.
[53] Article XIX.

While the division's composition of "different sexes and ages, so that the heavier parts may be performed by the stronger; the lighter by the more delicate individuals"[54] closely paralleled that of Fourier's ideal society,[55] his theory of the necessity for varying industrial occupations every two hours or about eight times a day[56] was not perpetuated in the Northampton Association's plans.

Fourier's first condition for successful associative labor, namely that every laborer be a partner in the enterprise, filled with the spirit of ownership and participation,[57] was carefully adhered to, and Article XXIII stipulated that every man, woman and child above the age of five years was to have a separate account with the Association. This account consisted of a record of the hours of labor contributed by each member. Annual settlements were to be held and the funds on hand were to be disbursed in the following order: "1st expense of stock transactions and management, including labor; 2nd expense of supporting members of the Industrial Association unable to earn a support; 3rd six percent on all stock actually paid in." The balance was to be divided among the members of the Industrial Association in proportion to their services with two-thirds allotted to labor and one-third to skill.[58]

The Preliminary Circular made only scanty provisions for communal living, possibly because the detailed descriptions of Fourier's "Phalanstery"[59] were inapplicable to the situation at Northampton. It was, however, stated that the board of industrial directors was to provide suitable employment for all members; to managae the purchase and sale of materials and goods for the Association and for individuals on a strictly cash basis; furnish members with accommodations at reasonable rentals, and domestic supplies at cost. This same body was also to serve as a board of arbitration to settle all difficulties between divisions, sub-divisions, or individuals; fix the rate of compensation for all ages and employments "awarding higher compensation to the most necessary and disagreeable rather than to the most productive" tasks.[60] No charge was to be made to any member for religious or other instruction, for medical attendance or nursing by members of the Association; and members were free to employ the services of non-members for such attention—at their own expense. Public rooms, baths, "or whatever is provided for the general use and benefit, unless used for some private or particular purpose" were also free to all.[61] Members

[54] Article XXI.
[55] Fourier, *op. cit.*, p. 155-162.
[56] *Ibid.*, p. 164.
[57] *Idem.*
[58] Article XIV.
[59] Fourier, *op. cit.*, p. 137-154.
[60] Article XVIII.
[61] Article XXII.

who were expelled from the society, or wished for personal reasons to withdraw were to receive all payments due them from both stock and labor at the next annual settlement, provided that they served ninety days' notice of their intentions and signed a full discharge of all claims against the Association.[62]

Final provision was made in the Circular for the alteration of any, or all, of the articles at a regular meeting of the Association by a majority of two-thirds of the members, provided that such alterations were in strict accord with the provisions of the by-laws and were not inconsistent with the "spirit and intention" of the declaration.[63]

Appended to the Articles of Association in the Preliminary Circular there was an announcement to the effect that the owners of the property known as the Northampton Silk Factory Estate had unanimously approved of the Articles, and were willing to place their property at the disposal of the projected Association as soon as $50,000 worth of stock was subscribed and $30,000 paid up.[64] This was signed by Joseph Conant and William Adam in their official capacities as officers of the Company, and was followed by a statement approving of the Declaration of Sentiments to be subscribed to and signed by prospective stockholders.[65]

There we evidently little doubt in the minds of the founders that their Preliminary Circular would bring quick results and within a month preparations were being made for the stimulation of the community's intellectual life as the following letter from W. L. Garrison to George Benson dated March 22, testifies:

> I shall endeavor to visit Northampton on my way . . . and . . . I intend if I can, to add Wendell Phillips to our company. . . . So, you may make your arrangements . . . for at least one "incendiary" meeting in your place.[66]

Such a feeling of hopefulness has not, however, been unanimous among the members of the Company, and shortly after the Preliminary Circular was published William Coe decided to withdraw from the experiment. He relinquished his rights, amounting to "one undivided fourth" of the joint holdings, to William Adam on February 26, for $2,000.[67] The records do not reveal any reason for Mr. Coe's withdrawal, and it can only be surmised that having joined the original venture for purely financial reasons he had no interest in the forthcoming Association, or at least, not sufficient faith in its outcome to feel justified in taking the economic risk. Joseph Conant,

---

[62] Article XVI.
[63] Articles XXIV and XXV.
[64] Sheffeld, *op. cit.*, p. 73.
[65] *Idem.*
[66] Garrison, *op. cit.*, Vol. 3, p. 49.
[67] *Hampshire County Record Book*, Vol. 95, p. 16-17.

the other member of the Company whose primary concern was with financial success,[68] elected to remain with Benson, Hill and Adam in the new venture. He had been in charge of the silk factory since early in 1839,[69] had full confidence in the future of the business,[70] and in addition he may have seen in the Association's provisions for employment of its members a welcome local solution to the labor shortage problem which at this time was affecting all of New England as a result of the increasing volume of western emigration.[71]

April 8, 1842 found some forty-one persons (twenty of whom were children) registered as members of the Northampton Association of Education and Industry.[72] Although the $30,000 in paid up stock, which had been established as a minimum for organization, was far from realized[73] the first official meeting of the Association was held at Boughton's Meadows, with the following charter members in attendance: Joseph Conant, Erasmus D. Hudson, G. W. Benson, Theodore Scarborough, Hiram Wells, E. D. Swift, and William Adam.[74] At this meeting a Constitution was adopted, and Joseph Conant was appointed president, Samuel L. Hill, treasurer; and William Adam, secretary of the Association.[75]

Later that same day (April 8, 1842) Conant, Hill and Adam "in consideration of $1 and other valuable and adequate consideration" conveyed the Silk Company Estate (the title to which was free and clear with the exception of a $15,000 mortgage to Charles N. Talbot; $6,000 of which was due on May 1, 1842)[76] to George Benson,[77] who in turn made over the property for the same considerations to Conant, Hill and Adam, "as they are Trustees of the Northampton Association of Education and Industry . . . and are to use the land for the . . . interests and purposes declared and set forth in the Articles of Association . . . a copy of which is hereinto annexed."[78] The Articles were in reality the Constitution and By-laws which

[68] William Adam in a letter to John Bailey dated March 16, 1843, in the *Book of Letters of the Northampton Association of Education and Industry;* quoted in Sheffeld, *op. cit.,* p. 85.

[69] See Chapter II.

[70] *The Northampton Courier,* May 26, 1841.

[71] New York State Agricultural Society, *Transactions I,* (1841), p. 359; quoted in P. W. Bidwell and J. I. Falconer, *History of Agriculture in Northern United States: 1620-1860,* (Washington, 1925), p. 274.

[72] Association's *Secretary's Book,* quoted in Sheffeld, *op. cit.,* p. 103-105.

[73] Mrs. Judson, "Northampton Association of Education and Industry" in *Macdonald MS,* p. 67-70; original in Yale University Library, photostat copy in possession of author. Also quoted in John H. Noyes, *History of American Socialisms* (New York, 1870), p. 156; further statement in Hill letter, *op. cit., Hampshire Gazette,* April 2, 1867.

[74] *Journal* of the Association, quoted in Sheffeld, *op. cit.,* p. 74.

[75] *Ibid.,* p. 80.

[76] *Hampshire County Record Book,* Vol. 93, p. 73.

[77] *Idem.*

[78] *Ibid.,* Vol. 95, p. 230-231.

had been unanimously adopted at the Association's first official meeting, and recorded in the *Journal of the Northampton Association of Education and Industry*.[79]

The Constitution had been drawn up by the founders who in their discussions found themselves almost without exception in accord as to their hopes, aspirations and ideas for the evolvement of the experiment. They sought "the development of a true social and moral life; advancement in truth and goodness, promotion of a general intelligence and liberal religious sentiments."[80] They shared, in common with the founders of other Associative movements of the early 1840's, a conviction that life as manifested in the organization of society at large was untenable; and their protest against the usages of that society resolved itself into a movement calculated, so they thought, to dissolve the problems of social chaos in the placid waters of utopian socialism. The Constitution which they produced, save for its insistence upon two distinct companies to conduct the affairs of the Community (a scheme for which no precedent seems to appear in the organization of other socialistic communities), was not unique.

The preamble clearly reflected the Quaker inheritance of both Benson and Hill in its defamation of "the governments of the world (which) are systematically warlike in their constitution and spirit, in the measures they adopt, and in the means they employ . . . to redress their real and alleged grievances, without regard to truth, justice, or humanity;" and its insistence upon the evil of combining for "the purpose of war, aggression, conquest, tyranny and enslavement" in contrast to the advocation of "Fair argument as . . . the only legitimate means of controlling the opinions or belief of another"; and the maintenance that "no reward or punishment ought to be awarded for any opinions or belief for which every human being is responsible to God alone."

The strong abolitionist sentiments of the majority of the members were equally clearly reflected in the document, but perhaps the most prominent and bitter denunciation of existing social phenomena was reserved for an expression of the religious convictions of the "Reformist" members of the group. It was their contention that:

Religion, whose essence is perfect spiritual liberty and universal benevolence, is prostituted into a device for tyrannizing over the minds of men by arraying them into hostile sects, by substitution of audible and visible forms for the inward power of truth and goodness, and by rendering superstitious fear and irresponsible dictation of men paramount to the veneration and authority that belong only to God.[81]

---

[79] Quoted in Sheffeld, *op. cit.*, p. 74-80; also in *Hampshire County Record Books*, Vol. 95, p. 233-240.

[80] Hill letter, *op. cit., Hampshire Gazette*, April 2, 1867.

[81] Preamble, Constitution of 1842.

They were further convinced that:

> to combine for the purposes of spreading speculative doctrines and ceremonial observances, forms of religious worship and discipline is injurious to the welfare of mankind, because . . . (they cause) the outward show of religion to take the place of its practical and spiritual influences, and to afford an instrument to priests and tyrants to enslave the mind and body.[82]

Despite the preponderance of anti-formalistic dogma which is found in the Constitution, the Northampton Association cannot be called a religious community in the generally accepted sense of the term. Their revolt against conventional religion, while calling down upon the Association the opprobrium of the surrounding countryside as subversive of true Christianity, did not result in any consolidation of views as was the case at the Hopedale Community; not was it characterized by any "new" religion such as Mormonism.

However advanced their views on religion may have been, the founders were strongly conservative in their views on the institution of the family:

> The family relation, the relation between the husband and wife, and between parents and children, has its foundation and support in the laws of nature and the will of God, in the affections of the heart and the dictates of the understanding. Other and wider relations may be formed for the purpose of social improvement, but none that are inconsistent with this which is sacred and permanent. . . .[83]

This attitude was in marked contrast to Fourier's advocation of "free divorce" and "a new domestic Order where marriage no longer exists."[84]

The desire for the elevation of labor to its true dignity, so clearly expressed in the Preliminary Circular, was reiterated in the Constitution. The statement was made that it was not only the right but also the duty of all to combine for the purpose of giving labor its just rewards;[85] which Fourier[86] and the Associationists agreed could never be acquired under the conventional system of distribution.

The aura of Transcendentalism which had pervaded the Preliminary Circular was by no means as dominant in the Constitution. Its influence, however, was not entirely lacking, and its strongest reflection appeared in the insistence upon the eqality of all without distinction of sex, color or condition; and that there be:

> full enjoyment of liberty in thought, in word, and in action; . . . promoting the progressive culture and full development of all the capacities of

[82] *Ibid.*, Article VII.
[83] Preamble, Constitution of 1842, Article VI.
[84] Fourier, *op. cit.*, p. 77-81.
[85] Preamble, Constitution of 1842, Article I.
[86] Fourier, *op. cit.*, p. 181-189.

human nature by the union of spiritual, intellectual and practical attainments.[87]

Through this development all were to "endeavour to discover and to adopt purer and more salutary principles, and to apply them individually and collectively to the regulation of their conduct of life" in order that the Association might succeed in correcting "the manifold evils of society and promote its further progress."[88]

The Constitution added little to the details of the organization of the stock company which had been set forth at such length in the Preliminary Circular. It did, however, stipulate that:

The Stock Directors may attend the meetings of the Industrial Directors, and give their advice, but shall not be allowed to vote.[89]

and the Industrial Directors were accorded the same privilege in the Stock Directors' meetings. Persons who had paid three-fifths of their pledged subscriptions were granted admission to the organization, and were entitled to vote.[90] Further provisions were made that stock might be paid for in some equivalent of money at the option of the Stock Directors, and persons without capital who were judged suitable for admission to the Community were allowed to subscribe for stock and pay for it out of their earnings as members.[91] Non-capitalistic members were not, however, to be allowed to vote until such time as they succeeded in paying for the prescribed three-fifths of their stock indebtedness.[92]

The only great difference in economic policy between the Preliminary Circular and the Constitution appeared in Article XXIII of the latter document. This Article stated in part:

after the actual payments of stock shall amount to thirty-one thousand, two hundred dollars, they (the Trustees) shall have no power as officers and agents of the Community to buy or sell on credit.

This provision was of extreme importance for the future development of the Association. For, by empowering the Trustees to buy or sell on credit *until* the stock payments reached $31,200, it flatly nullified the specific provision in Article IV of the Preliminary Circular that "The Trustees shall not have the power to buy or sell, as agents of the company, on credit." This destruction of one of the cardinal principles of the Community's economic philosophy constituted a compromise between the ideals of the founders and the hard facts of the Association's financial position, as according to the

---

[87] Preamble, Constitution of 1842, Article VII.
[88] Preamble, Constitution of 1842.
[89] Constitution of 1843, Article III.
[90] *Ibid.*, Article IV and VIII.
[91] *Ibid.*, Article IX.
[92] *Idem.*

figures recorded in the *Macdonald MS*, only $20,000 had been paid in and there was already a debt of $11,000. Obviously, if the Association was to begin its life at all it would have to do so on a credit basis. However, in effecting this compromise the founders failed to erect any safeguards against over-expansion, or to establish any plan which would enable them to work directly toward their original goal. The mere adoption of credit as a basis for financial operation was in itself a wise move. But it was the application of the policy without foresight or moderation that led down the path to destruction.

The provisions in the Constitution for the welfare and development of the Industrial Community were hardly more detailed than those of the Preliminary Circular. Some innovations were introduced, and Article XXVI stated that if the Industrial Community could not supply the type of labor required for some Associative project from its own membership, outside labor might be hired for that specific purpose at the expense of the Community at large. If on the other hand, members could not be provided with employment or preferred some type of work not offered by the Industrial Association, they were perfectly free to seek outside employment under the condition that all remuneration received for their services was to be expended for the benefit of the Association. Members were, however, required to live on the lands belonging to the Community.[93]

The question of arbitration of disputes was elaborated under Article XXX, which gave a clear picture of the procedure to be followed:

Any matter in dispute shall be decided by arbitration. The two parties concerned shall each select an arbitrator. The two arbitrators thus selected shall chose a third, and the three thus chosen shall constitute a Board of Arbitration, who shall in open court hear the representations and examine the witnesses of both parties, and shall deliver a written decision, comformable to equity and good conscience, which shall be binding without appeal, and shall be placed on record for future reference and guidance. The arbitrators shall be compensated for their time and labour by the Association according to a rate fixed by the Industrial Directors.

Any violations of this regulation by recourse to law courts of the outside world, either instead of employing the suggested method of arbitration or as an attempt to have the decisions of the Board of Arbitration set aside, were to be punished by expulsion from the Association.[94]

Charles Fourier, in outlining what he believed to be the elements constituting a perfect location for an Associative community or, as he termed it—a Phalanstery, had written:

The land should be provided with a fine stream of water; it should be intersected by hills, and adapted to varied cultivation; it should be

[93] Constitution of 1842, Article XXVIII.
[94] Constitution of 1842, Article XXXI.

contiguous to a forest, and not far removed from a large city, but sufficiently so to escape intruders.[95]

To the casual observer the property of the Northampton Association must have appeared as an almost literal realization of this ideal, albeit on a small scale. The Association itself, however, was by no means so closely patterned after Fourier's model Phalanx. In the first place, the Northampton Association, like Brook Farm and Hopedale, its contemporaries in the venture into the uncharted waters of utopian socialism in Massachusetts,[96] started its life with only a handful of members, where Fourier envisioned some 1,500 or 1,600 as a basic minimum.[97] In the second place, its social and economic organization while following Fourier's outline in part, differed greatly in the emphasis placed upon the various departments. The founders in their personal views, and in the public expression of the Association's aims in its Preliminary Circular had proclaimed themselves in effect to be in agreement with Fourier's attitude toward the organization of economic society in the world at large:

> The mechanism of commerce is organized in opposition to common sense. It subordinates the social body to a class of parasitic and unproductive agents, the merchants. All the essential classes, the proprietor, the cultivator, the manufacturer, and even the government, find themselves dominated by an accessory class, that of the merchant . . . which, nevertheless, directs and obstructs at its pleasure all the forces of circulation.[98]

However, while Fourier's Phalanstery was based upon a predominantly agraraian society which regarded manufacturers "as a means of diversion in . . . the long winter vacation and the equatorial rains,"[99] the Northampton Association focused its social and economic organization around manufacture. The founders were no doubt influenced by the fact that the presence of an established industry had played a large part in the Community's inception and possibly by the philosophy of William Adam's fellow Scotchman, Robert Owen, which maintained that "MECHANISM AND SCIENCE will be extensively introduced to execute all the work that is over-laborious, disagreeable, or in any way injurious to human nature."[100]

The Silk Factory had not completely ceased operation during the period of transition from private enterprise to socialistic venture, and quite logically one of the first acts of the newly created industrial community was to establish a Silk Department, and to place at its head Earl Dwight

---

[95] Fourier, *op. cit.*, p. 139.
[96] Noyes, *op. cit.*, p. 16-17.
[97] Fourier, *op. cit.*, p. 138.
[98] *Ibid.*, p. 99-100.
[99] *Ibid.*, p. 138.
[100] Robert Owen, *A New View of Society and Other Writings*, (New York, 1927), p. 229.

Swift[101] who had served as factory foreman under both the Northampton Silk Company[102] and the Conant[103] regime. The first concern of the Stock Directors was also for the continuation of the factory's production and they immediately purchased a quantity of raw silk[104] from their President, Mr. Conant, who evidently had not placed all his assets at the Association's disposal.

OLD OIL MILL, THE FIRST FACTORY OF THE NORTHAMPTON SILK CO. Redrawn by C. L. Gethman from the painting by C. C. Burleigh, Jr.

The Mechanical Department, under Joseph Conant, and the Lumber Department, under Samuel Brook's direction, were the next divisions to be organized.[105] Their facilities were already in condition for immediate use and consisted, according to a statement in the Preliminary Circular, of a water wheel; saw mill; Raymond's shingle mill, capable of turning out some 10,000 shingles per hour, for which the patent right—making the Association the only licensed manufacturer of these shingles in Northampton—had been secured; a planing machine for planing and jointing boards, planks and timber; as well as a variety of smaller mechanical tools such as a turning lathe, circular saws, etc. In addition, the Association possessed a fifty acre pine forest located near the saw mill.[106]

[101] *Journal* in Sheffeld, *op. cit.,* p. 81.
[102] Brockett, *op. cit.,* p. 52.
[103] Northampton *Courier,* May 26, 1841.
[104] *Journal* in Sheffeld, *op. cit.,* p. 81.
[105] *Idem.*
[106] *Hampshire County Record Book,* Vol. 92, p. 270.

George Benson was placed in charge of the Agricultural Department[107] as he previously managed large farms in Brooklyn and Providence.[108] The selection of a person of experience to manage this unit was a wise and, indeed, an imperative step, for the Agricultural Department was perhaps the poorest yet organized from both the point of material possessions and ultimate prospects. Provisions had been made at the second meeting of the Association on April 9th for the purchase of farm tools, ten or twelve cows, one yoke of oxen, six horses, pigs and chickens,[109] a necessary but at the same time an expensive step. A large portion of the land was planted with mulberry trees, and the rest, while moderately fertile, had been impoverished by intense cultivation of both mulberry trees[110] and sugar beets.[111]

Personal acquaintance, or a probationary period, as pre-requisites to admission to full membership seem to have been requirements in almost all of the socialistic communities,[112] and the Northampton Association was no exception.[113] This custom helps to explain the fact that the name of Hall Judd appears together with those of Samuel Brooks and George Benson as a member of the Board for the admission of new members[114] although, according to the *Secretary's Book*, Judd did not become a full member until May 28, 1842.[115] A similiar situation existed in the case of David Mack, who was appointed as a Director of the Stock Company at the first meeting of the Association together with Benson, Theodore Scarborough,[116] and Swift, although in actuality he did not formally join until May 15th when his name and those of his wife and two children were entered in the *Secretary's Book*.[117] Hall Judd was the first Northampton man to join the Community. He was a son of Sylvester Judd, the publisher of the *Hampshire Gazette* from 1832-1834 and an anti-slavery sympathizer.[118] Little is known of the younger Judd, but his father writing of him in a journal on August 20, 1843 remarks: ". . . Hall is stubborn in his ways, conscientious but an infidel,"[119] and in another entry written in 1850 after the son's death:

When he (Hall) changed some of his views and opinions, on religious, social, and other subjects, he well knew that some of his former friends

---

[107] *Journal* in Sheffeld, *op. cit.*, p. 81.
[108] Sheffeld, *op. cit.*, p. 67.
[109] *Journal*, Sheffeld, *op. cit.*, p. 81.
[110] Mr. Hill in a letter to the *Hampshire Gazette, op. cit.*, April 2, 1867.
[111] *Hampshire Gazette*, July 1, 1840.
[112] Noyes, *op. cit.*, p. 103.
[113] Sheffeld, *op. cit.*, p. 103.
[114] *Journal*, Sheffeld, *op. cit.*, p. 80.
[115] *Secretary's Book*, Sheffeld, *op. cit.*, p. 104.
[116] *Journal*, Sheffeld, *op. cit.*, p. 80.
[117] *Secretary's Book*, Sheffeld, *op. cit.*, p. 104.
[118] Files of the *Hampshire Gazette*, 1832-1834, *passim*.
[119] Judd, Sylvester, *Memorabilia*, ed. by Arethusa Hall (Northampton, 1882), p. 129.

would grow cool; that he should be esteemed wild, foolish, etc.; but influenced by principle, he did not trouble himself about these things.[120]

David Mack, who was destined to play an influential part in the development of the Association, was a son of "General" David Mack of Amherst.[121] He had attended Williams College, had been graduated from Yale with the class of 1823 and, after his marriage to Lucy Maria Kollock Brastow in 1835, spent several years studying law with his uncle Judge Elisha Mack of Salem, Massachusetts.[122] Although he was admitted to the Bar,[123] he seems not to have devoted much of his time to practicing law. Turning to the field of education, he established a school for girls first in New Bedford,[124] and then in Cambridge[125] where evidently he became acquainted with the Transcendentalist group, and through them actively interested in experiments in socialized living. In 1841 he had contemplated joining George Ripley's community at Brook Farm, even going so far as to sign his name to the original "Articles of Agreement" of that association.[126] He was, however, dissuaded from taking the final step of membership. It has been suggested that his acquaintance with Nathaniel Hawthorne may have influenced his decision not to join the Brook Farm community.[127] Hawthorne was among the first members to live and work at Brook Farm, and his reaction to the situation there as reflected in a letter to David Mack, dated July 18, 1841, did not paint a very attractive or encouraging picture of the community's prospects.[128] Hawthorne admitted that his views varied somewhat with the state of his spirits, but he had spoken "very despondently, perhaps desparingly of the prospects of the situation" to Mack at their last meeting and in the letter he reiterated that his hopes for success were "never, of late, very sanguine." In reaching this conclusion Hawthorne says:

I form my judgment, however, not from anything that has passed within the precincts of Brook Farm but from external circumstances— from the improbability that adequate funds will be raised or that any feasible plan can be suggested for proceeding without a very considerable capital.[129]

David Mack's connection with the Northampton group less than a year

[120] *Ibid.*, p. 138.
[121] The Northampton *Courier*, August 23, 1843.
[122] E. M. Treman & M. E. Poole, *The History of the Tremon, Tremaine, Truman Family in America*, (Ithaca, N.Y., 1901), p. 380-382; 439.
[123] *Ibid.*, p. 439.
[124] Manning Hawthorne, "Hawthorne and Utopian Socialism," in the *New England Quarterly*, Vol. 12, 1939, p. 726.
[125] The Northampton *Courier*, August 23, 1843.
[126] Lindsay Swift, *Brook Farm*, (New York, 1908), p. 18; also John T. Codman, *Brook Farm* (Boston, 1894), p. 15.
[127] Hawthorne, *op. cit.*, p. 726.
[128] *Ibid.*, p. 727-729.
[129] *Ibid.*, p. 727-728.

later reveals both his sincere interest in the Associative movement, and the fact that the Northampton Community's seemingly solid economic basis had convinced him that its chances for ultimate success were superior to those of Brook Farm. He was, indeed, so sure that the Northampton Association would prove successful from all points of view, that after a very short acquaintance with the Community (probably before he himself became a full member) he endeavored to enlist Hawthorne as a member. Hawthorne had resigned his membership in the Brook Farm experiment in the fall of 1841, and at the time he replied to Mack's invitation to join the Northampton Community he was probably already making arrangements to move into the Old Manse in Concord, for his marriage occurred barely six weeks later.[130] This letter written by Hawthorne to Mack on the 25th of May, 1842, would seem to indicate, however, that he had given at least some serious consideration to the possibility of joining the Northampton group:

When I last met you I expressed my purpose of coming to Northampton in the course of the present month in order to gain information as to the situation and prospects of your community. Since our interview, however, circumstances of various kinds have induced me to give up the design of offering myself as a member. As a matter of conscience, with my present impressions, I should hardly feel myself justified in taking such a step; for though I have much faith in the general good tendency of institutions on this principle, yet I am troubled (after my experience of last year) whether I as an individual am a proper subject for these beneficial influences. In an economical point of view, undoubtedly, I would not do so well anywhere else; but I feel that this ought not to be the primary consideration. A more important question is, how my intellectual and moral condition, and ability to be useful, would be affected by merging myself in a community. I confess to you , my dear Sir, it is my present belief that I can best attain the higher ends of my life by retaining the ordinary relation to society.[131]

Had Hawthorne joined the Northampton Community its daily activities and some of its personalities might well have appeared in his writings in much the same manner that his Brook Farm experiences was reflected in the *Blithedale Romance*; and his membership would undoubtedly have attracted greater and more widespread attention to the Association. All of this is of course purely conjencture, but it is true that the dearth of information about the Northampton Association is largely due to its lack of literarily articulate members, (such as Adin Ballou proved to be for Hopedale, and John Thomas Codman for Brook Farm) and to the fact that its membership was made up of men and women from middle class society who had no accomplishments to make them figure conspicuously in the public eye.

[130] Hawthorne, *op. cit.*, p. 729.
[131] *Ibid.*, p. 729-731.

The months of April and May, 1842, were a period of development for the Northampton Association. Membership in the little group rose from forty-one to sixty-five,[132] and theories and provisions of the Circular and Constitution were slowly and, sometimes painfully, transformed into reality. It became apparent, almost at once, that one of the greatest oversights in the preparation for communal living, from a practical point of view, had been the failure to make specific provision at the time of organization for the accommodation of any large number of members and their families. The five frame dwelling houses already standing on the property[133] were hardly more than sufficient for the immediate needs of the founders and their families; and the influx of new members, some of whom were not attached to family groups, created a serious housing problem.[134] Obviously something had to be done about this situation before the community could begin to function smoothly and effectively. The quickest solution to the problem seemed to lie in the conversion of a brick building which had originally been a wool warehouse.[135] The Factory Boarding House, as the building soon came to be called, was fitted up for its new role as rapidly and as inexpensively as possible; and in consequence presented a very unfinished appearance as all the partitions were constructed from plain boards, and the entire building was lacking in the conveniences to which most of the members had been accustomed at home.[136] Furthermore, it was not purely a residential building as the Community laundry was located in the basement, two rooms on the second floor were given over to some of the silk machinery, leaving only a bunk room on that floor for the single men, while the third floor was entirely taken up by the Community Store and more machinery belonging to the Silk Department. The fourth floor was divided into apartments for family use,[137] apartments so small that they seem to have been designed with Fourier's injunction in mind that in the "new Order" members should not remain at home, except in case of illness.[138] According to the reminiscences of some of the earlier members, a large part of the group who took up residence in the Factory Boarding House when it was first opened were relatives and being already intimately acquainted did not mind the lack of privacy as much as might have been expected.[139] Some of the parents were anxious because of the danger from fire in the rudely constructed building, and others disliked having their apartments so far from the ground for fear that the children would fall out of the windows.[140] On the

---

[132] *Secretary's Book,* in Sheffeld, *op. cit.,* p. 103-105.
[133] Hampshire County Record Book, Vol. 84, p. 380-383.   ..
[134] Mr. Benson in statement quoted in Noyes, *op. cit.,* p. 156.
[1.5] Sheffeld, *op. cit.,* p. 59.
[136] Francis P. Judd, "Reminiscences," quoted in Sheffeld, *op. cit.,* p. 116.
[137] Sheffeld, *op. cit.,* p. 82.
[138] Fourier, *op. cit.,* p. 195.
[139] "When I Was a Girl" in Sheffeld, *op. cit.,* p. 123.
[140] George R. Stetson, "When I Was a Boy" in Sheffeld, *op. cit.,* p. 120.

whole, however, one and all were willing to undergo privations and make sacrifices so that the Community might prosper.[141]

Mr. and Mrs. Hiram Wells were appointed as managers of the Boarding House and were given explicit instructions to provide accommodations for only "such boarders as the Stock Directors might sanction."[142] This provision was probably made to safeguard the Association against the prolonged visits of relatives or curious visitors which had proved to be such a source of expense to the Brook Farm Community.[143] After a short time it became obvious that some regulations were necessary for the comfort and economy of those living in the Boarding House, and the following rules were adopted at a meeting of the Association in June:

1st. All boarders are required to retire to their sleeping apartments for the night at one half past nine o'clock, and to extinguish their lights at ten o'clock.

2nd. It is left exclusively to the discretion and judgment of the superintendents of the Boarding House to make provision for the table and generally for the comfort and convenience of the boarders, and in the event of any dissatisfaction of the boarders they are requested to first make known their wishes to the superintendents, and finally, if necessary, to the Board of Industrial Directors.

3rd. Washing is included in "Board and Lodgings" to be furnished by the Association, but should any boarder appear at the end of the year to have occasioned disproportionate expense on this account he will be debited with the excess.

4th. Mending is not included in "Board and Lodging," and the boarders are left to provide for their own wants in this respect, either through the Department of Domestic Economy, in which the charges will be as moderate as will compensate for the labour, or in any other way that may be preferred.[144]

There was no compulsion placed upon the members to move to the Boarding House and, while many continued to live in the available private homes, (which the founders' families seem to have shared so generously with as many of the other members as could be accommodated) the five frame dwellings located near the Boarding House could only accommodate limited numbers so that the majority were Boarding House residents. A very real inducement to communal living presented itself in the fact that board and lodging cost about fifty cents a week in contrast to the seventy-five cents to a dollar for the same period in private homes.[145]

Once the Community's housing problem had beeen settled, another problem presented itself, namely that of wages. There was a prolonged

[141] Hill letter, *op. cit., Hampshire Gazette*, April 2, 1867.
[142] Sheffeld, *op. cit.*, p. 82.
[143] *Codman, op. cit.*, p. 96.
[144] *Journal* in Sheffeld, *op. cit.*, p. 83-84.
[145] Hinds, *op. cit.*, p. 278; also Hill letter, *op. cit.*, in *Hampshire Gazette*, April 2, 1867.

discussion of the matter at several community meetings,[146] but the final decision was made to postpone the announcement of any wage scale until the annual settlement in January.[147] This resolution may have been influenced by the fact that the Association did not have any too plentiful a supply of ready cash.[148] This decision had far reaching consequences in that it virtually forced the members of the Community, as well as the Community itself to do business on a credit, rather than a pay-as-you-go basis.

Having settled or postponed its most pressing problems and gotten its major departments into running order, the Association turned its attention to matters which had seemed less important, or at any rate, whose demands had been less pressing at the outset. Mr. Conant was authorized to purchase groceries "according to his best judgment for the use of the Community,"[149] and a store was established where members could purchase supplies of all varieties on credit.[150] Hall Judd, the clerk,[151] kept a strict account of the individual purchases, and the accounts were to be settled at the end of each year when the Association put its books in order. The store was a non-profit organization, articles being sold to members at cost in accordance with the provision made in the Constitution.[152] The following excerpt from the store's account book testifies to the fact that Departments (such as the Boarding House) made purchases from the store as well as the individual members:[153]

Sam A. Bottum, Dr.
   to ½ doz. eggs at 10¢   .05

Mary Ann Smith, Dr.
   to 1 Back Comb   .03

David Mack, Dr.
   to 50 Herring at ½¢   .25

Geo. A. Hill, Dr.
   to 1 neck collar   .20

Boarding House, Dr.
   to ½ doz. Britannia Spoons at 10¢   .83

Among the main objects in establishing the Association had been a desire on the part of the founders to initiate a liberal system of education which would afford better schooling for their children than could be ob-

---

[146] Sheffeld, *op. cit.*, p. 83.
[147] Sheffeld, *op. cit.*, p. 83.
[148] Hill letter, *op. cit.*, in *Hampshire Gazette*, April 2, 1867.
[149] *Journal* in Sheffeld, *op. cit.*, p. 108.
[150] *Idem.*
[151] *Idem.*
[152] Article XXVIII, Constitution of 1842.
[153] *Store Account Book* in Sheffeld, *op. cit.*, p. 106.

tained in the outside world.[154] As most of the families in the Community had several children it soon became feasible to organize a regular school program. Classes were held in a room in the mechanical department, and special slates and books were provided for an infant school.[155] Professor Adam, who in May had been appointed to prepare a course of lectures on Social Economy "in illustration of the principles and practices of the Association," was elected Director of the Educational Department.[156] He insttuted a program which united study and labor, thus carrying out the founders' Fourieristic[157] conviction that "no education . . . was complete which did not combine physical with mental development."[158] A special unit for the manufacture of raw silk and the care of the silkworm had been started,[159] and the children, under the supervision of Mr. O. D. Paine, the Director,[160] performed most of the work in this department. The boys carried in the mulberry leaves from the orchards while the girls distributed them along the various shelves in the cocoonery.[161] In the class room their studies consisted of instruction in literature, science, and moral and spiritual culture,[162] and here as in the cocoonery boys and girls worked side by side.[163]

Article I in the Preamble to the Constitution had stated that "Productive labour is the duty of every person," and when the first months of adjustment were over life in the Community began to take on regular pattern. Everyone worked together. "There was no high, no low, no masters, no servants, no white, no black"[164] but a common brotherhood striving for a common goal. The women occupied themselves at all sorts of domestic tasks, some were teachers in the school and others worked in the Silk Factory, some of the men were also employed there while others found employment on the farm, in the lumber and mechanical departments and still others took charge of some of the classes in the school.[165] There was much to be done if the Community was to prove self-supporting and the hours of labor were necessarily long. Those who worked in the Silk Factory were required to put in a twelve hour day,[166] and as all labor, in so far as it

---

[154] Hill letter, *op. cit.*, in *Hampshire Gazette*, April 2, 1867.
[155] Sheffeld, *op. cit.*, p. 83.
[156] *Journal* in Sheffeld, *op. cit.*, p. 81.
[157] Fourier, *op. cit.*, *passim*.
[158] Mr. Benson quoted in Noyes, *op. cit.*, p. 157.
[159] *Journal* in Sheffeld, *op. cit.*, p. 82.
[160] *Idem.*
[161] "When I Was a Girl," *op. cit.*, p. 124-125.
[162] Hill letter, *op. cit.*, in *Hampshire Gazette*, April 2, 1867.
[163] See footnote 161 above.
[164] Frederick Douglass, "What I Found at the Northampton Association," in Sheffeld, *op. cit.*, p. 130.
[165] Sheffeld, *passim*.
[166] "Reminiscences," *op. cit.*, p. 116.

was possible, was equally apportioned it may be inferred that this was the standard working day for the whole community. Nevertheless, time was found for evening gatherings of the Community in the school for lectures by members or visitors; simple parties or song gatherings; and smaller groups frequently gathered in various members' rooms for serious discussions of slavery, religion and a host of other topics.[167] There seems to have been very little intercourse between the Community and the town of Northampton in the early days for no reference of a social nature to either the Association or its members appears in any local paper until 1843. Hall Judd operated what was termed the "Daily Express between Broughton Meadows and the village of Northampton" and was credited with two hours of labor by the Association for undertaking this task. For a short time this service was charged for at the rate of "One cent per letter, one-half a cent per newspaper, two cents for an errand or business in which the use of a wagon is required,"[168] but within a month this charge was abolished[169] in order that the service might be equally available to all members. A fact which testifies that individual members were not in the habit of making frequent and regular trips to Northampton.

The silk business continued to be the most important single concern of the Association's economic life, and late in the summer of 1842 when forty or fifty pounds of raw silk were being used in manufacture of thread, ribbon and vesting every week the Community found that it was unable to produce through its own efforts a sufficient quantity of raw silk to supply the demand.[170] In order to obtain the necessary raw material to keep the factory producing at top speed the following advertisement was inserted in the local papers:

TO SILK GROWERS. Mr. O. D. Paine at the Silk Factory, Northampton will purchase on account of the Northampton Association, Raw Silk of good quality, at $4.50 per lb., and Cocoons of good quality at $3.00 per bushel, to be paid in manufactured silk, boards, shingles, or wood, or cash in part. He will also receive cocoons to be reeled, or silk to be manufactured on shares or for cash. . . .[171]

The repeated references to terms in barter in preference to cash would seem to indicate that the department did not have too generous a supply of ready cash. This indication that the Silk Business was not prospering was substantiated by the radical change which took place within the Association during the following two months.

On August 24, 1842, Conant and Adam transferred the Community's property to Benson and Mack, and this deed included a new purchase of

---

[167] "Old Community Times" in Sheffeld, *op. cit.*, p. 115-135.
[168] Sheffeld, *op. cit.*, p. 83.
[169] *Ibid.*, p. 84.
[170] Hill letter, *op. cit.*, *Hampshire Gazette*, April 2, 1867.
[171] *Hampshire Gazette*, August 9-23, 1842.

some fifty more acres known as "Hough Hill" which was mortgaged for $1,564.28.[172] Following the change of Trustees, Mr. Swift resigned as director of the Silk Department;[173] and on October 8th, Mr. Conant and his wife withdrew from the Association.[174] They were followed in rapid succession by Swift and Orwell S. Chaffee with their families.[175] There are several possible reasons for the action which Conant, Swift and Chaffee took. The first is that some of the more zealous "laborite" members of the Association had objected to the fact that the members who were employed in the Silk Factory were required to work twelve hours a day, and by expressing themselves to be seriously against this labor policy they had been successful in effecting a reduction of one hour per day. In the words of a member of the Community: "The immediate consequences of this proceeding were injurious to the financial interests of the Association . . . (of this) . . . there is no doubt."[176] The second reason which may have influenced Conant and his friends to withdraw lay in the fact that although the Community was already heavily burdened with mortgages still other obligations of this nature were being incurred.[177] The third and undoubtedly the strongest reason for their action was the fact that Conant was already negotiating for some near-by property on which he was planning to start a Silk Factory of his own.[178] Chaffee and Swift had originally come to Northampton at Conant's suggestion. All three were related[179] and it was only natural that they should decide to withdraw from the Community when he offered them an opportunity to form an independent partnership[180] which promised more personal financial gain than they could hope to achieve by remaining a part of the Associative movement.

The loss of three such valuable men who had contributed the knowledge of years of practical experience in the silk business was a very real blow to the Association's future economic prospects and caused it temporary financial embarrassment through the withdrawal of their shares of stock.[181] However, the members, officially at least, chose to regard the loss in quite a different light as can be seen in this letter written by Professor Adam early in 1843.

. . . The fact is that towards the close of last year three of our members left us, finding that they had hastily united with us, and they could or would not merge their private interests in the general and common interest. The separation has taken place in an amicable way. They are all three

---

[172] *Hampshire County Record Book,* Vol. 100, p. 154-155.
[173] *Journal* in Sheffeld, *op. cit.,* p. 84.
[174] *Ibid.,* p. 103.
[175] *Ibid.,* p. 103-106.
[176] "Reminiscences," *op. cit.,* p. 116-117.
[177] *Hampshire County Record Book,* Vol. 100, p. 154-155.
[178] *Ibid.,* Vol. 97, p. 51; also Northampton *Courier,* August 22, 1843.
[179] *Book of Letters* in Sheffeld, *op. cit.,* p. 85.
[180] *Hampshire Gazette,* December 12, 1843.
[181] Sheffeld, *op. cit.,* p. 36.

relatives, have commenced business and purchased farms in our immediate neighborhood, have received from us all the assistance which it has been in our power to give, and have given us all the accommodation in their power in withdrawing their stock. They are men of good private character as the world goes, but their object in joining appears to have been from the first pecuniary advantage, not moral improvement, or social usefulness, and we feel that their departure has strengthened us instead of weakened us.[182]

The Hampshire, Franklin and Hampden Agricultural Society in its Annual Report on October 18, 1842 announced that the first prize premiums for both raw silk and sewing silk had been awarded to the Northampton Association, and remarked in addition that their sewing silk was "a superior article—the colors brilliant and the silk every way well made."[183] Cheered by this report, an influx of new members, and numerous applications for membership[184] which soon lifted the burden imposed by the withdrawal of Conant, Swift and Chaffee, the Community recovered rapidly from its shock and set about organizing a cutlery and a shoe making department,[185] and in general preparing for the new year which they hoped would open a period of greater prosperity.

[182] See note 179 above.
[183] The Northampton *Courier*, October 18, 1842.
[184] Shffeld, *op. cit.*, p. 86.
[185] *Idem.*

CHAPTER III

EXIT THE COMMUNITY

The first "Annual Meeting" of the Northampton Association of Education and Industry was an occasion to which its members must have looked forward with eager and anxious hearts. The little group of social pioneers had laboured for nine months in the colony at Broughton's Meadows and this meeting was their initial opportunity to take stock of their achievements and to obtain a well rounded picture of the development of the experiment to which they had subscribed their efforts, their talents and their money. Many problems involving both policy and practice had arisen during the nine months they had worked together, problems which had been deferred for settlement until the annual meeting in the hope that by that time they might be resolved more expediently out of the wisdom of experience. The bulk and seriousness of these matters was so great that they could by no means be settled at a single session, and the annual meeting for 1843 became, perforce, a series of meetings fitted into the daily routine whenever it was convenient and possible for the entire Community to gather together; and although these sessions were held from January 20 until February 1,[1] all the items of business on the agenda were not even then decided to the satisfaction of the majority of the members of the Association.[2]

Undoubtedly the matter which was of the deepest personal concern to all was the determination of a basic hourly wage for labor performed within the Community. The Directors had specifically postponed the settlement of this question until the annual meeting because at the beginning of the experiment they had neither the funds to operate on a pay-as-you-go basis, nor any estimation of the productivity or expenses of the Community which would have enabled them to resolve the matter immediately.[3] The time had now come for a decision. The members, together with the directors, studied the Secretary's record of the individual hours of work contributed by every member of the Association over five years of age.[4] Next, they consulted the storekeeper's account of the items purchased on credit by individuals and by the various departments.[5] Following this, they reached an agreement that proportionate deductions should be made for every hour spent away from the community during working hours, on business not authorized by the Association.[6] They finally determined upon

[1] Sheffeld, *op. cit.*, p. 87.
[2] *Ibid.*, p. 93; also *Hampshire County Record Book*, Vol. 100, p. 355-369.
[3] Rumsey, *op. cit.*, p. 25; Sheffeld, *op. cit.*, p. 83.
[4] Articles 6-7 of the Preliminary Circular.
[5] *Idem*, and Sheffeld, *op. cit.*, p. 106.
[6] Excerpt from the *Macdonald MS* quoted in George K. Smart, "Fourierism in

a wage scale. This was to be adopted without any qualifications, despite the fact that at the time of the original postponement of the question of wages, explicit provisions had been made to the effect that they would consider "the actual nature, usefulness and value of the labor performed by each member."[7]

Children under 12 years of age	1¢ per hour
Children 12 to 16 years of age	3¢ per hour
Boys and girls 16 to 20	4½¢ per hour
Men and women over 20	6¢ per hour[8]

Even taking into consideration the relatively greater purchasing power of the dollar in that day, this was not a high wage, it was in fact one half to four cents below the average hourly rate then being paid to laborers in the Northampton area, as is illustrated by this chart:

Children under 12 years of age	2¢ per hour
Children 12 to 15 years of age	3¢ per hour
Boys and girls 15 to 17	5¢ per hour
Women over 17	6¢ per hour
Men over 17	10¢ per hour[9]

This condition would have been untenable had it not been for the ensuing alterations in the financial provisions of the Association's constitution. The document had originally stipulated that the members should be "credited with the value of labor performed, and charged at a reasonable rate with the rent of apartments . . . and at cost with articles for domestic consumption."[10] This was now changed so that every member was in the future to be provided with "food, lodging, necessary furniture, fuel, oil and clothing . . . at the public expense"[11] and to receive his wages in the form of an equal share in the net profits of the Association.[12] The removal of economic pressure from the individual eliminated the element of competition and bound up the interests of the members even more closely with those of the Association. The new provisions were put into operation through the adoption of standardized allowances, based on the actual cost to the Community of the various commodities.[13] A member discussing this system in later years stated that while the allowance for food and clothing was by no means liberal it was at least an adequate sum. Persons

---

Northampton: Two Documents," *The New England Quarterly,* Vol. XII, No. 2 (June, 1939), p. 374.

[7] Journal quoted in Sheffeld, *op. cit.,* p. 83.
[8] *Secretary's Book,* quoted in Sheffeld, *op. cit.,* p. 87.
[9] *Hampshire Gazette,* April 19, 1842.
[10] Article 28, Constitution of 1842.
[11] Resolution 3 from the *Macdonald MS* in Smart, *op. cit.,* p. 373.
[12] Resolution 4 from *Idem.*
[13] Resolution 3 from *Idem.*

over eighteen received twenty dollars a year for clothes; those between fourteen and eighteen, fourteen dollars; children from ten to fourteen, ten dollars; those between six and ten, eight dollars; and babies under six, five dollars.[14] Food allotments were eighty cents a week for all persons over ten, and forty cents for children under ten.[15] She further stated that on the whole families were able to get along more comfortably under this arrangement than single individuals, because the family allowance could be "lumped" together and spent as need or desire arose, while the individual had access only to the original amount designated for his use.[16] The revision was accompanied by social as well as economic repercussions, inasmuch as it had formerly been more expensive to live in a private dwelling than in the Community Boarding House,[17] a fact which must have caused a certain amount of social distinction and occasioned some hard feelings within the group. The establishment of a greater equality among the members through standardizing expenditures undoubtedly contributed to the peace of mind and harmony of all.

After these basic problems were settled, the attention of the annual meeting was turned toward the necessity for a further revision of the constitution. The original body of rules had been drawn up by a small group before the needs of the Community were fully known,[18] and while the founders had secured the best legal advice obtainable[19] in preparing this instrument, neither they, nor their advisors, had any practical experience in the direction of communal living and thus from the nature of the case could not have been expected to foresee and guard against many contingencies. The spirit which brought about the revision was in no sense hostile to the original design of the founders "to progress towards a better state of society,"[20] but was rather intended to "carry out that design more fully"[21] by creating an even greater equality of both rights and powers among the members, and by furnishing them with a still greater incentive for cooperation and labor.[22]

The preamble to the constitution was entirely rewritten, and the new version, instead of containing a broad statement of the general beliefs and convictions of the Association, confined itself to a discussion of the necessity of a more throughgoing adoption of the principle of equal brotherhood

[14] Sheffield, *op. cit.*, p. 90.
[15] *Idem.*
[16] Rumsey, *op. cit.*, p. 26.
[17] See above p. 48.
[18] See above p. 25.
[19] Sheffield, *op. cit.*, p. 83.
[20] S. L. Hill, *op. cit., Hampshire Gazette,* April 2, 1867.
[21] William Adam in a letter to Moses K. Meader dated February 27, 1843, in Sheffield, *op. cit.*, p. 88.
[22] *Macdonald MS* in Smart *op. cit.*, p. 373-374.

within the organization and stressed the fact that the application of this principle would permit:

"no distinction of rights or rewards between the strong and the weak, the skilful and unskilful, . . . the rich and the poor . . . never accord to property peculiar privileges, but make the earth . . . the common heritage of the race as *one great family* . . . welcoming all to an equal participation."[23]

These phrases, which reflected a closer affinity with the doctrines of Charles Fourier by their emphasis upon "Unity" and "Familism" which he considered to be the true basis of a perfect socialist society,[24] constituted an unequivocal nullification of the provisions in the original document to the effect that "disbursements (of the annual net profit) shall be made (by) two-thirds . . . being awarded to labor, and one-third to skill,"[25] that "The Stock directors shall determine in what manner . . . funds shall be invested" and business carried on;[26] and that "a person without capital . . . shall not be entitled to vote . . . or to receive dividends."[27] The amendments effected by the remainder of the new constitution were perfectly in keeping with both the spirit and the intentions expressed in the preamble.

The first article did away with the strange feature of the Association's original structure, the existence of two distinct companies; one for the direction of Stock and the other for the direction of Industrial activities, and in their place created one sovereign body in which all capital:

Whatsoever contributed by individuals to stock should come under the exclusive management of the body thus associating, subject to no other interference . . . all having an equal voice in its regulation . . . recognizing no individual right . . . except that of the contributor upon withdrawal.[28]

The Northampton Association like many other Phalanxes[29] had adopted the plan, approved by Fourier,[30] of selling stock outside as well as within the Community with the result that trouble had arisen over the differences in interest between the two groups,[31] and this was obviously an attempt to resolve the dilemma in favor of the active members.

The interests of the body politic were further protected by another amendment which stipulated that each member was to have one and only one vote,[32] whereas under the old ruling it had been possible for a single individual to control, through stock purchases, as many as ten votes.[33]

[23] *Macdonald MS* in Smart, *op. cit.*, p. 372.
[24] Fourier, *op. cit., passim.*, Smart, *op. cit.*, p. 372.
[25] Article 29, Constitution of 1842.
[26] Article 20, Constitution of 1842.
[27] Article 9, Constitution of 1842.
[28] *Macdonald MS* in Smart, *op. cit.*, p. 373.
[29] Smart, *op. cit.*, p. 373.
[30] Fourier, *op. cit.*, p. 134 ff.
[31] Smart, *op. cit.*, p. 374.
[32] Article 1, Constitution of 1843.
[33] Article 15, Constitution of 1842.

Furthermore the voting age was raised from sixteen[34] to eighteen years[35] so that the well being of the community might not be endangered by the decisions of immature minds. This was a necessary safeguard because the provisions of the new constitution extended the power of the voting members of the Association so that they, rather than the stockholders, became responsible for the selection of the directors of the various departments,[36] and for the admission of new members.[37] These changes in the constitution were accepted at the annual meeting with relatively little dissent.[38] Three other and even more radical amendments were, however, so hotly contested[39] that the new constitution did not receive formal ratification until the following October.[40] The first of the disputed amendments established a ten hour working day for "all able bodied and healthy" members of the Association,[41] and met with the same objection which had been advanced when the basic working day had been changed from twelve to eleven hours during the summer of 1842,[42] namely, that it would reduce the Association's rate of productivity and preclude any possible financial profit.[43] The second point of contention arose over an amendment which specifically abolished the provision in the old constitution that had allotted one-half of the net annual profit to labor, one-fourth to capital and one-fourth to skill.[44] The objection here seems to have been that the new regulation, in providing for the distribution of one-fourth of the net profit equally among the members and the creation of a sinking fund with the remaining three-fourths,[45] was not liberal enough and many members disapproved of the creation of an Association fund.[46] The third and most serious[47] controversy was occasioned by an amendment which empowered the directors or the Community, acting as a body, to spend the Association's funds as they saw fit without first obtaining a vote of sanction from the stockholders.[48] This provision completely removed the jurisdiction over the Association's money from the hands of the stock directors where it had been originally placed.[49]

[34] Article 13, Constitution of 1842.
[35] Article 6, Constitution of 1843.
[36] Article 2, Constitution of 1843, and Article 4, Constitution of 1842.
[37] Article 5, Constitution of 1843, and Article 5, Constitution of 1842.
[38] William Adam to Moses K. Meader, *op. cit.*, in Sheffeld, *op. cit.*, p. 88.
[39] Letter written by Mr. Mack, dated July 22, 1843, in Sheffeld, *op. cit.*, p. 92.
[40] *Hampshire County Record Book*, Vol. 100, p. 360.
[41] Article 7, Constitution of 1843.
[42] See p. 53 above for a further discussion of this point.
[43] Frances P. Judd, "Reminiscences" in Sheffeld, *op. cit.*, p. 117.
[44] Article 29, Constitution of 1842.
[45] Article 4, Constitution of 1843.
[46] William Adam to Moses K. Meader, *op. cit.*, in Sheffeld, *op. cit.*, p. 88.
[47] As it occasioned Mr. Adam's withdrawal from the society, see p. 75 below.
[48] Article 1, Constitution of 1843.
[49] Article 20, Constitution of 1842.

Although the divergence of opinion over these matters prevented the immediate ratification of the revised constitution, it may be gathered from a letter written by Mr. Mack in July, 1843[50] that the more radical element was successful in obtaining a temporary adoption of the suggested provisions, a move which accomplished their aims, gave doubtful members an opportunity to observe the results of a practical application of the theory of equality but did little towards promoting a spirit of harmony within the community. As Mr. Mack stated:

> All our members *are not* satisfied with the modifications, and there exists among us a difference of opinion as to the propriety of continuing the modifications permanently, or of returning to the provisions of the Constitution, though I cannot persuade myself that we shall again ever consent to give votes to dollars.[51]

It was the issue of communal as opposed to capitalistic control of the Association's affairs which produced a rift between two of the original founders. Mr. Mack's statement quoted above together with the fact that he was elected to the Presidency[52] at the annual meeting would seem to indicate that he was strongly in favor of, if indeed not responsible for, the amendments to the constitution, while Mr. Adam protested strongly against these changes stating that he considered them to be: "illegal . . . contrary to the law of the land; and . . . immoral . . . (and) contrary to the plainest principles of justice and honesty."[53] It is interesting, however, to note that despite his clearly expressed disapproval of the constitutional changes, Mr. Adam remained firm in his sincere faith in the validity of the experiment. Writing in his capacity as Secretary,[54] in response to the flood of inquiries from friends and prospective members, be said:

> The result of one year's experience has been on the whole satisfactory to all concerned and although much pressed for capital we are advancing into the second year with increased energy and spirit.[55]

Even in private correspondence, although remarking that he considered the exclusive control by labor to be "exceedingly bad and imperfect,"[56] he was emphatic in stating that it was the opinion of the large majority of the Association that the amendments by investing "the whole body of the members with equal rights and powers . . . more fully . . . (united)

---

[50] Sheffeld, *op. cit.,* p. 92.
[51] Mr. Mack in a letter dated July 22, 1843 quoted in Sheffeld, *op. cit.,* p. 92.
[52] *Macdonald MS, op. cit.,* p. 72.
[53] Mr. Adam in a statement to the Stockholders, September 30, 1843, quoted in Sheffeld, *op. cit.,* p. 93.
[54] *Macdonald MS, op. cit,,* p. 72.
[55] Mr. Adam in a letter quoted in Sheffeld, *op. cit.,* p. 91.
[56] Mr. Adam in a letter to H. G. Wright, Feb. 17, 1843, quoted in Sheffeld, *op. cit.,* p. 88.

them in cooperative industry and . . . (gave) them a common interest in the produce of their labor."[57]

The dissent occasioned by the constitutional amendments seems to have had relatively little effect outside the Association as applications for membership flowed in in an increasing stream;[58] and the Community was given ample opportunity to exercise its new power concerning the admission of members as their numbers grew from 102 (of which 30 were men over 18, 26 women and 46 children under 18)[59] to 180 within a year.[60] The basis for the selection of new members seems never to have been clearly defined, and consequently it was inevitable that social drones, those persons who had never been able to earn a living under the circumstances of the outer world, were attracted to the Community where capital and labor shared and shared alike and no distinction was made between stockholder and non-stockholder. Another type of person whose admission to the group was of questionable wisdom was the inventor who more frequently than not was possessed of little else save his invention and the latter, as the Association all too frequently learned to its sorrow and expense, was apt to be worthless.[61] There were, of course, still others who sought to join because of a sincere faith in the tenets of the Transcendentalist and Fourieristic beliefs which had instigated the foundation of the Community, and as time wore on, the Association came to realize that it was "more highly important to select members who . . . were interested in realizing the undertaking of the Association, especially their moral and social undertakings, and in making money."[62] The only precaution taken, however, seems to have been the continuance of the requirement for personal acquaintance[63] before admission to full membership, and under this regulation many persons were provisionally accepted into the Community for probationary terms of two, six or twelve months.[64]

The social composition of the Association was predominantly middle class[65] although all walks of life were represented in the membership, and, as "no distinction was made on account of color,"[66] teachers, blacksmiths, businessmen, ministers and carpenters,[67] both black and white, labored and lived side by side in friendship and with mutual respect.[68]

---

[57] Mr. Adam in a letter to M. K. Meader, Feb. 27, 1843, quoted in Sheffeld, *op. cit.*, p. 88.
[58] Sheffeld, *op. cit.*, p. 90-91.
[59] Letter quoted in *ibid.*, p. 92.
[60] *Hampshire Gazette*, August 29, 1843; also November 13, 1843.
[61] Rumsey, *op. cit.*, p. 26; Hinds, *op. cit.*, p. 276; Sheffeld, *op. cit.*, p. 93.
[62] Mr. Mack in a letter dated July 22, 1843; quoted in Sheffeld, *op. cit.*, p. 92.
[63] See p. 31 above for further discussion of this point.
[64] Sheffeld, *op. cit.*, p. 91.
[65] Hinds, *op. cit.*, p. 277.
[66] "Reminiscences," *op. cit.*, p. 117.
[67] Sheffeld, *op. cit., passim.*
[68] *Idem.*

There is nothing in the records of the Association to indicate the number of negroes who joined the group, but it is evident from remarks made by (other) members in their recorded reminiscences,[69] and from casual references in the local press,[70] that there were several of them living at the community. The most outstanding representatives of this group of members were David Ruggles, Frederick Douglass, and Sojourner Truth. Ruggles was an elderly, blind colored man who had been associated as a youth with the Quaker Isaac T. Hopper in the underground railroad.[71] Douglass at the time he came to the Northampton Association had only recently escaped from slavery and was just starting out in his career as an abolitionist lecturer.[72] Sojourner Truth, the only negro woman ever mentioned in connection with the Association, was a colorful figure; she had been born in Africa and after being brought to this country was held as a slave in New York State and after buying her freedom had been active as an evangelist.[73] She came to New England with the thought of going to Bronson Alcott's "community" at Fruitlands but friends in Springfield advised her to go to Northampton instead.[74] Here although, as is related in the story of her life:

> She did not fall in love at first sight with the Northampton Association for she arrived there at a time when appearances did not correspond with the ideas of associationists as they had been spread out in their writings. . . .[75]

she became a devoted and hard working member, loved and respected by all for her quaint way of speech, ready wit and sterling character.[76]

The industrial development of the Association was materially aided by the growth in membership and 1843 saw the establishment of four new departments—Silk growing, Store, Accountant and Secretarial—the conversion of the oil mill into a grist mill and the construction of a large cocoonery.[77] The influx of new life was equally stimulating to the growth of the Association's social and intellectual interests, and the general stabilization of the routine duties of communal living that accompanied the second year gave greater opportunity for cultural activities. A book club and a library were organized, a special reading room was established in the factory building and a lyceum started.[78] The lyceum meetings were held

[69] Sheffeld, *op. cit.*, p. 116-135.
[70] *Hampshire Gazette*
[71] "What I Found at the Northampton Community," *op. cit.*, p. 131.
[72] *Ibid.*, p. 130-132.
[73] *Narrative of Sojourner Truth* (Boston, 1850), *passim*.
[74] *Ibid.*, p. 114.
[75] *Narrative of Sojourner Truth, op. cit.*, p. 115.
[76] Sheffeld, *op. cit.*, p. 117-135, *passim*.
[77] *Ibid.*, p. 90-91.
[78] *Idem.*

regularly during the winter months in the dining room of the Community Boarding House, and a variety of programs was presented. Sometimes the children recited pieces and the singing classes gave recitals. More frequently members of the Association engaged in "spirited debates," or distinguished visitors such as William Lloyd Garrison and Wendell Phillips addressed the gathering;[79] and occasionally the Community was entertained by professional talent such as the then famous singers of the Hutchinson Family.[80] More informal evenings were spent in dancing, candy pulls or card parties[81] when time and energy permitted.

Simplicity seems to have been the key note of life in the Northampton Association, a simplicity which must have been born out of conviction as well as privation. One member writes of a wedding celebrated at "the breakfast table of the factory dining hall, with no cake or cards but brown bread and wooden chairs and a Squire to make the rite legal."[82] This same spirit carried through in all aspects of their dealings, and the officers of the Community and their families received no special accommodations and were accorded no special privileges. Mrs. Mack scrubbed floors, while Mrs. Adam and her daughters "engaged in occupations, which once, while residing in India, were performed for them by 18 servants."[83] Many other members, particularly among the women, had been accustomed to more comfortable surroundings and lighter tasks than those they found to be their lot at the Community. That the housekeeping arrangements of the Association suffered in consequence of their inexperience, is testified to by an excerpt from the journal of Elihu Burritt, "the Learned Blacksmith," in which he says:

> I . . . set out . . . to visit Prof. Adam . . . it procured me an ocular demonstration how utterly impractical, unnatural, visionary and absurd was this chimerical species of Association. . . . The apartments I visited were cold, comfortless & untidy. Accomplished ladies who had left good homes & the luxuries of refined life, were here surrounded by their half abandoned children, trying to learn the trade of some factory operative . . . with all the respective provisions of such a character, scattered around in slattern profusion & negligence.[84]

Despite this unflattering picture, and the fact that there was a certain amount of jealousy between the workers and the intellectuals[85] in the group, and not infrequent arguments about the equality of the distribution of the work,[86] on the whole the members got on together as well "as

[79] Sheffeld, *op. cit.*, p. 96.
[80] John W. Hutchinson, "The Hutchinson's Visit" in Sheffeld, *op. cit.*, p. 132-135.
[81] *Macdonald MS, op. cit.*, p. 69.
[82] G. D. Stebbins, "A Young Man in the Community" in Sheffeld, *op. cit.*, p. 127.
[83] Merle Curti, *The Learned Blacksmith* (New York, 1937), p. 17.
[84] *Ibid.*, p. 16-17.
[85] Hinds, *op. cit.*, p. 277.
[86] Sheffeld, *op. cit.*, p. 94.

is usual in good neighborhoods"; and although their social life was admittedly "unconventional going to the bounds of propriety but not beyond"[87] there were no scandals or acts of violence within the Community at any time.[88] It is evident however, from the emphatic manner in which an article published in the *Gazette* and *Courier*[89] denied that the Association was "a company of Fourierites,"[90] despite the "incorrect notice which . . . (had been) going the rounds,"[91] that some attacks had been made upon the morality of the Community; inasmuch as Fourier's advocation of the abolition of formal marital ties[92] seems to have been the primary target for social critics of the period.[93]

If the attacks upon the Association's moral atmosphere were made without foundation in truth, the Community's religious life was sufficiently unconventional to provide ample material for comment, especially in a town whose religious traditions included the teaching of Jonathan Edwards. The Northampton Association had from the first, in accordance with the convictions of its founders, been insistent in its "protest against sectism and bigotry . . . (and in its) assertion of the paramount importance of human brotherhood."[94] Therefore, religion, or its lack, had not formed any part of the qualifications for membership[95] and the group included "many . . . with Quaker ideas . . . thinking all days alike holy;[96] those of no religious bias or profession;[97] a Catholic priest";[98] and some representatives of the various protestant denominations.[99] The manner in which the Association chose to observe the Sabbath gave further affront to the surrounding countryside which already considered them "visionary, fanatical and foolish."[100] Their meetings were held in the dining room of the factory building during the winter months,[101] and under a "gigantic old pine tree" on the grounds in the summer.[102] Instead of a regular religious service the meetings took the form of discussions at which as a member once told an inquiring divine:

---

[87] "A Young Man in the Communtiy," *op. cit.*, p. 126.

[88] *Idem;* also no reports in any of the newspapers, or other accounts of the Association.

[89] *Hampshire Gazette,* August 29, 1843; Northampton *Courier,* August 23, 1843.

[90] *Idem.*

[91] *Idem.*

[92] Fourier, *op. cit.*, p. 76-81.

[93] Donald C. M'Laren, *Boa Constrictor or Fourier Association Self Exposed,* (Rochester, 1844), p. 20-28.

[94] "What I Found at the Northampton Association," *op. cit.*, p. 130.

[95] See p. 25 above for a further discussion of this point.

[96] "Reminiscences," *op. cit.*, p. 116.

[97] "What I Found at the Northampton Association," *op. cit.*, p. 130.

[98] "When I Was a Boy" in Sheffeld, *op. cit.*, p. 122.

[99] See note 97 above.

[100] "Reminiscences," *op. cit.*, p. (115).

[101] Sheffeld, *op. cit.*, p. 96; also G. D. Stebbins, *op. cit.*, p. 127.

[102] *Idem.*

We all speak if we wish, men and women. You can come and say what you please; we will treat you well, but we may not agree with you and may ask questions.[103]

Usually they dealt with "subjects of a religious nature, and individuals were afforded an opportunity to develope their peculiar views upon religion and education."[104] If the following excerpt from the *Hampshire Gazette* can be assumed to be illustrative of the regular conduct in these gatherings, it becomes apparent that the Community services were open to all who cared to attend, and guests as well as members were apt to be freely criticized for their beliefs.

A MORMON: We understand that one of Jo Smith's disciples held forth at the 'Community' in this town last Sabbath. After he had stated his belief, a member of the Community got up and exposed the fallacy of the Mormon system.[105]

Noted men such as Wendell Phillips, George Thompson, Henry C. Wright, and William L. Garrison were frequently invited to address the group at its Sunday[106] gathering, and the presence of such well known personalities in addition to the unusual character of the meetings occasioned notice even outside of Northampton. *The Massachusetts Whig*, a Springfield paper, even went so far as to send a special correspondent to one of the services and his report gives perhaps the best and most complete picture of "Sunday at the Community":

. . . after sitting some time in silence which was broken by a spontaneous effusion of singing, W. L. Garrison read a chapter from the New Testament, which as adapted to the occasion represented them as struggling with difficulties on all sides in carrying out their principles. . . . As this was the last time he was meeting with them he took the occasion to give them an address. . . . Not indeed did he declare himself an unreserved advocate of their principles but merely expressed his feeling hopes of them as having associated in an experiment to benefit mankind and to retrieve a ruined world. . . . As he might take it for granted that the members were generally Anti-Slavery, Anti-war and Temperance men.
There was an interval of impressive silence, interrupted in the meantime by an outburst of vocal devotion.
Reference was made to the subject of discussion in the last meeting. . . . The question was, the authority of the Bible for the observance of the Sabbath, and other ordinances of the Christian Church. . . . Prof. Adam opened the discussion. He considered the doctrine of some, that all laws of duty were absolutely written within the hearts of men, as erroneous and of bad tendency. Reason, that it would degenerate into mere self will. . . .

[103] "A Young Man in the Community," *op. cit.*, p. 127.
[104] Excerpt from *The Massachusetts Whig* published in the *Hampshire Gazette*, November 14, 1843.
[105] *Hampshire Gazette*, July 25, 1843.
[106] Sheffeld, *op. cit.*, p. 96.

But the opposite opinion was satisfactorily supported by Messrs. Garrison and Boyle. . . . The opinions as to the moral state of man in the fall was elicited on some remarks from Boyle. . . . Garrison occupied an immense portion of the latter part of the meeting, (which held near 3 hours). (He said that when man reached the perfect state and society there would be no need for Sunday as) every day itself will afford its proportional period of mental and religious exercise and of respite from the toils of the body.[107]

Evidently the Association's insistence upon the themes of anti-clericalism and anti-sectarianism had come to be construed as a downright opposition to the church itself, and quite naturally this aroused the ire of Northampton's more circumspect citizens;[108] and this, together with the Community's espousal of the Abolitionist cause, seem to have been the chief sources of the criticism and opprobrium heaped upon it by the local press.[109]

Adam, Benson and Mack were all very active in the Abolition movement, having been appointed representatives of the Latimer Committee of Boston early in 1843, and authorized to call an anti-slavery convention in Hampshire County for the purpose of choosing two delegates to present a petition against slavery to the Massachusetts legislature.[110] Professor Adam seems to have been particularly interested in the cause and spent some time in attending abolition meetings throughout the state. On one occasion he presided at a convention held in Manchester, Connecticut, and the Northampton *Courier* in reporting the incident managed, by way of editorial comment, to give its opinion of his activities in no uncertain terms:

Prof. Adam of Northampton, a British Subject, presided at an Anti-Slavery Convention . . . where it was resolved 'that the compact between the North & the South is the great political support of slavery, involving the North equally with the South, in the guilt of slave holding, *and that it is the duty of the free States peaceably to withdraw from the Union* (sic.)' Should a resolution be passed by a political meeting in England to subvert the government, and an American preside over such an assemblage, what would be the public sentiment in regard to him, and what the probable consequences to him?[111]

The *Gazette* was no more charitable in its version of a service conducted by the members of the Association in celebration of the anniversary of the West India slave emancipation, for, despite the fact that the gathering was held in the auditorium of the First Church, the *Gazette* remarked:

The character of most of the signers to the call, led people to believe that

[107] Excerpt from the *Massachusetts Whig* reprinted in the *Hampshire Gazette*, November 14, 1843.
[108] *Hampshire Gazette*, August 8, 1843.
[109] *Hampshire Gazette* and Northampton *Courier* 1843-1847 *passim*.
[110] *Hampshire Gazette*, January 23, 1843.
[111] Northampton *Courier*, March 7, 1843.

it was to be a church-denouncing meeting, and as they didn't care to hear themselves abused, they stayed away. . . . A colored man was put in the chair. This was not in very good taste or, at any rate, was not so regarded in this town. . . . Professor Adam occupied the forenoon in the first address . . . (he) was succeeded by a colored man, who has recently escaped from slavery. Such speeches—if speeches they may be called—can do no good.[112]

Undoubtedly the Community's interest in the anti-slavery cause was stimulated by the presence of William Lloyd Garrison as a frequent guest. He spent several weeks there during the summer of 1843 resting at the home of his brother-in-law, George Benson,[113] and took advantage of every occasion to express his abolitionist views. It is interesting to note that the people of Northampton were no more receptive to his enthusiasm and eloquence than they had been to that of the Associationists, and Sylvester Judd, one-time editor of the *Gazette,* wrote in his diary on July 4, 1843:

Mr. Garrison and Mr. Boyle held forth on abolition. These men are too vituperative and denunciatory of almost everybody to do the greatest good.[114]

Towards the close of the year duties other than the work of carrying forward the cause of abolition, kept the leaders of the Association busy away from the Community. Mr. Mack and Mr. Benson began a series of lectures and conventions in central and western New York State, while Mr. Boyle canvassed the middle and eastern sections of Massachusetts, and Mr. Adam went to New York City and Philadelphia "to make arrangements with a publisher to print a literary article for the benefit of the Association."[115] Financial distress was the motivating force for this activity. No stock subscriptions had resulted from the efforts of the Community's representative, Henry C. Wright, in his tour of England,[116] and so the decision had been made to attempt to raise at least $25,000 by appealing to the friends of social reform throughout New England and New York State.[117]

There had been a good deal of shifting about of responsibility during the early spring: Mr. Mack had resigned the presidency and has been succeeded by Mr. Benson; while Mr. Adam had resigned both the secretaryship and the direction of the Educational Department, and these duties were assumed by Mr. Mack.[118] In August the trusteeship of the Association

---

[112] *Hampshire Gazette,* August 8, 1843.
[113] Garrison, *op. cit.,* Vol. 3, p. 82-83; also *Hampshire Gazette,* August 22, 1843.
[114] Sylvester Judd, *op. cit.,* p. 52.
[115] Sheffeld, *op. cit.,* p. 94; also mentioned in a letter from William Adam to D. L. Child dated October 3, 1843 found among the MS of the *Garrison Collection* in the Boston Public Library.
[116] Rumsey, *op. cit.,* p. 28.
[117] Sheffeld, *op. cit.,* p. 93-94.
[118] Sheffeld, *op. cit.,* p. 91.

was transferred by Mr. Adam and Mr. Conant, (who had evidently retained this position despite his withdrawal from the Community almost
a year before) to Benson and Mack. The deed of transfer recorded a balance
of $9,564.28 due on mortgages[119] and, since only about $20,000 was
actually invested in the project, there was a considerable debt.[120] Regardless
of this fact the Community plunged ahead into larger business ventures,
erecting a cocoonery, starting a grist[121] mill, and sinking a considerable
amount of money in a new type of wagon that proved to be impractical.[122]

Furthermore, the silk department which had shown signs of promise
towards becoming a profitable and self-supporting industry and whose
products had already found a good local market,[123] was now faced with
serious competition. By the middle of August, 1843, Mr. Conant had his
factory, located between the village of Northampton and the Community,
in operation[124] and the Northampton *Courier* reported on August 22 that
Mr. Valentine, an English silk dyer, was about to build another silk factory
in the locality.[125] This meant that the Association was faced with the
three fold problem of securing a sufficient quantity of raw silk to supply
its machines, of keeping the quality of the manufactured silk superior to
that of their competitors, and of holding their market. The gravest of these
problems was perhaps that of securing raw silk as the Association had
already been forced to advertise widely and indeed to purchase a considerable amount from foreign markets.[126] Undoubtedly the new cocoonery
was built in the hope that their supply could be substantially augmented
at home for they in all probability felt that competition would force the
price of raw silk up and the Association was in no position to pay out more
than they had in the past. The necessity of producing a superior grade
of manufactured silk was also a matter of great concern because Mr. Conant
was a man with wide experience in the silk business and he had the added
advantage of knowing the weaknesses of the Community's product at first
hand. Mr. Valentine, the other prospective competitor, was a master crafts-
man in the art of silk dying[127] and had indeed taught the Association's
dyemaster, J. D. Atkins, a former printer, all that the latter knew about
the trade.[128] Evidently the Community was successful in keeping up the
quality of their product because the American Institute of New York

---

[119] *Hampshire County Record Book*, Vol. 100, p. 154.
[120] Rumsey, *op. cit.*, p. 27; Sheffeld, *op. cit.*, p. 101; Macdonald MS, *op. cit., p.* 68.
[121] Sheffeld, *op. cit.*, p. 91.
[122] Rumsey, *op. cit.*, p. 26.
[123] Northampton *Courier*, August 22, 1843.
[124] *Idem.*
[125] *Idem.*
[126] "When I Was a Girl," *op. cit.*, p. 125.
[127] Brockett, *op. cit.*, p. 134.
[128] Sheffeld, *op. cit.*, p. 86.

awarded them a diploma for the best raw silk, and a second prize for their sewing silk, at the New York exhibition in 1843.[129] The adoption of a new and efficient method of reeling the raw silk from the cocoons, made possible by Mr. O. D. Paine's invention of a superior reeling machine,[130] also gave the Community the chance to produce better manufactured silk more cheaply than their competitors.[131] However, it is obvious from later developments that the prospects of the Association's silk department were seriously affected by the two new factories.

If the outlook for the Northampton Association's development had been, economically speaking, dubious at the end of its first nine months of existence, the beginning of 1844 found them in a considerably more serious condition as there was a debt of $30,000 and only $17,000 was invested,[132] due to the withdrawal of some members who had been disappointed in their expectations of great and immediate financial gain.[133]

The new year also brought the resignation of Professor Adam, the second of the original founders to withdraw from the Association. Mr. Adam's reasons for leaving the Community were in a sense the same as those of Mr. Conant, namely financial, but they were founded upon a distrust of the basic principles of the Association's economic philosophy rather than upon the desire for personal aggrandizement. The Professor, as has been stated, had been among those who objected to the re-writing of the Constitution in 1843. He had in fact felt so strongly about the matter that before the formal ratification of the new Constitution by the Community took place he had issued a letter of formal protest in which he reiterated his original dissatisfaction with the amendments and went on to say that he protested:

in particular, as a direct violation of the constitution of law and of morality, against the assumption, whether by individual members of the association holding office, or by the Industrial Community in their associated capacity, of the power to appropriate the funds of the Association for any purpose whatsoever without the sanction, either of a regular vote of the stockholders, or of the Directors appointed by them as their representatives.[134]

This serious and considered protest seems to have had little if any effect upon the Community for after further debate the new Constitution was adopted by the Stock Company on October 15, 1843 and by the Industrial Community on October 28.[135] The new rulings went into effect officially

---

[129] Brockett, op. cit., p. 122.
[130] Hampshire Gazette, October 24, 1843.
[131] Idem.
[132] Sheffeld, op. cit., p. 101.
[133] Sheffeld, op. cit., p. 85-101.
[134] Letter from William Adam to the Stockholders of the Northampton Association, copied in the Association's Record Book and quoted in Sheffeld, op. cit., p. 93.
[135] Hampshire County Record Book, Vol. 100, p. 355-360.

on January 1, 1844,[136] and on January second Mr. Adam, his wife and their three daughters withdrew.[137] They went to live in the "John Rogers homestead" on Elm Street in Northampton,[138] where, having severed his connection with the Community, Mr. Adam became popular in the town's intellectual circles, giving several lectures in the lyceum series on his favorite topics "England in India" and "The Philosophy of History"[139]; while his daughters conducted a "select boarding school for young ladies" at their home[140] for some time before the family's removal to Chicago[141] in 1847.

At the time of Mr. Adam's resignation from the directorship of the Association's education department in April 1843, Mr. Mack and his wife had assumed the duties of that office and instituted even more liberal methods and standards.[142] Instead of long hours of classroom study the children were taken out into the woods and fields to learn their botany and biology at first hand from nature,[143] and they were taught "to build the different geographical formations, miniature islands, capes, promontories, peninsulas, and isthmuses" on the banks of Mill River,[144] or taken by carriage[145] to Mt. Holyoke in search of mineral specimens.[146] The superiority of these "oral and practically illustrated" lessons, the excellent teachers and the fact that corporal punishment was not allowed attracted attention to the Community school.[147] Many parents who were not members wished to have their children educated there, and a boarding school was started to accommodate them.[148] The tuition, which did not include books, clothing or stationery, was set at one hundred dollars for the school year and the money went directly into the Association treasury.[149] The "Boarders" were required to join in the work of the Community to the same extent as the children of members, and after a long morning—the usual class hours were from seven to twelve—passed in academic pursuits, they spent the remainder of the day from one until sunset at various tasks involving manual labour.[150] Boys and girls both worked in the Cocoonery,

---

[136] *Idem.*
[137] List of members, *Secretary's Record Book* quoted in Sheffeld, *op. cit.*, p. 103.
[138] *Hampshire County Record Book*, Vol. 104, p. 74.
[139] Northampton *Courier*, March 4, and 11, 1845.
[140] Advertisements in the *Hampshire Gazette;* various dates during 1845.
[141] *Hampshire County Record Book*, Vol. 104, p. 75.
[142] "When I Was a Girl," *op. cit.*, p. 124.
[143] *Idem.*
[144] "When I Was a Boy," *op. cit.*, p. 121.
[145] Association *Account Book*, quoted in Sheffeld, *op. cit.*, p. 106.
[146] "When I Was a Girl," *op. cit.*, p. 124.
[147] Letter from G. W. Benson to S. J. May, January 20, 1844, Garrison Collection, *op. cit.*
[148] Sheffeld, *op. cit.*, p. 95.
[149] *Idem.*
[150] Sheffeld, *op. cit.*, p. 95.

and in the winter months they were taught "sewing, braiding straw, knitting silk and beaded purses and other useful[151] things" while the director or teacher in charge of the work read aloud from "Shakespeare's plays, Scott's novels, Prescott's 'History of the Conquest of Mexico,' Undine and many other . . . books."[152] In between their hours of work and study the children somehow managed to find plenty of time for skating, climbing trees, fishing, swimming and playing, and all those who wrote of their childhood at the Community in after years seem to have enjoyed and profited from their experiences there.[153]

The initial popularity of the boarding school encouraged the directors, and having in mind perhaps the great success of the school at Brook Farm,[154] they made several attempts to secure a prominent educator to assume the leadership of the Northampton Association's educational department. Early in the year Mr. Benson entertained some hope of persuading Mr. Alcott to come to Northampton, and in writing to a friend mentioned the fact saying ". . . If Mr. Alcott should come . . . we have it in contemplation of hiring . . . a large house adjoining our premises for the better accommodation of the Educational Department."[155] Evidently this plan came to nothing for in December Mr. Benson wrote to the Reverend Samuel J. May and offered him the position stating that undoubtedly "an arrangement (could be made) upon pleasant and agreeable terms" if Mr. May would "take charge and direct a school the profits of which should go to support the Association," and that he (Mr. Benson) felt sure that enough pupils could be secured if a suitable director was in charge.[156] This proposal must have been declined because there is no further reference to the matter in the Association's records and the school continued under the direction of Mr. Mack.

The prospects of the school as a source of revenue were encouraging, but not sufficiently concrete to offset the fears produced by the Association's general economic condition. Even Mr. Benson, who in January, 1844 had written to a friend that "we have met thus far with good encouragement and are making arrangements to extend our business and commerce building the coming season,"[157] became so discouraged by the Community's steadily growing debt that he despaired of the groups ability to liquidate it and in June offered to buy up all the stock and property of the Associa-

---

[151] "When I Was A Girl," *op. cit.*, p. 124.
[152] *Idem.*
[153] "Old Community Times," *op. cit.*, p. 115-135, *passim.*
[154] Swift, *op. cit.*, p. 69-85, *passim.*
[155] Letter from Mr. Benson to Rev. S. J. May dated January 20, 1844 in the *Garrison Collection, op. cit.*
[156] Letter from G. W. Benson to Rev. S. J. May dated December 23, 1844 in the *Garrison Collection, op cit.*
[157] Letter from G. W. Benson to Rev. S. J. May dated January 20, 1844 in *Ibid.*

tion at cost and to assume its liabilities.[158] The Community as a body, however, did not share his views of the hopelessness of the situation and after some little deliberation rejected the offer.[159] There is no record of the factors which influenced this decision to continue the experiment in the face of ever growing odds, but it can be safely conjectured that the increased activity of the society of "Friends of Social Reform" may have been among the determining factors because at a meeting of this group held at Hopedale in May every encouragement had been given to the associative movement and promises of mutual aid had been made by the three Massachusetts communities.[160]

"The Friends of Social Reform" society had been organized by George W. Benson and fourteen others at a convention held at Worcester, Massachusetts, in December 1843 for the purpose of "reorganizing society into Associations or Communities in which all may have a *common interest*."[161] This meeting was followed by a series of lectures on the subject of associationism in Worcester and Leominster,[162] and a week later David Mack, G. W. Benson, J. N. Buffum, H. C. Wright and others issued a call for a convention of the society in Boston.[163] The Boston gathering occasioned considerable comment in reformist circles and William H. Channing wrote in *The Present* for January 15, 1844, that:

it marked an era in the history of New England. It was the commencement of a public movement upon the subject of social reform, which will flow on wider, deeper, stronger. . . .

The Convention was organized by the choice of William Bassett of Lynn, as President, of Adin Ballou, of Hopedale, G. W. Benson of Northampton, George Ripley of Brook Farm and James N. Buffum of Lynn as Vice Presidents. . . . It is a pleasure to express gratitude to Charles Fourier, for having opened a whole new world of study, hope and action.[164]

In order to facilitate "the advance of the Social Scheme discovered by Charles Fourier"[165] and to allow the associations "to concert means to actualize their idea"[166] plans were laid for Brook Farm, Hopedale and Northampton each to send two delegates to a series of three meetings to be held every year at the respective communities in rotation.[167]

---

[158] Sheffeld, *op. cit.*, p. 94; Rumsey, *op. cit.*, p. 27.
[159] *Idem.*
[160] Ballou, *op. cit.*, p. 131-132.
[161] Ballou, *op. cit.*, p. 131-132.
[162] *The Practical Christian* quoted in Ballou, *op. cit.*, p. 119.
[163] *Idem.*
[164] Quoted in Noyes, *op. cit.*, p. 513.
[165] Quoted in Noyes, *op. cit.*, p. 513.
[166] *The Practical Christian* quoted in Ballou, *op. cit.*, p. 119.
[167] *Ibid.*, p. 131-132.

Neither Benson nor Mack attended the first of these conferences which was held at Hopedale on May 24, 1844,[168] although they had been primarily responsible for starting the society. The records give no explanation of this fact but it is possible that it was necessary for these gentlemen to devote their energies to the lecture field at this time inasmuch as the Northampton Association was still attempting to bolster its economic foundations by canvassing for stock subscriptions. Brook Farm was represented by George Ripley, its founder, and Ephriam Capen, while Butler Wilmarth and Adin Ballou, the founder of Hopedale, were its delegates and James Boyle and Josiah Hayward formed the Northampton contingent.[169] At the meeting a thorough investigation was made of "the statistics, resources, industrial arrangements, methods of education, and particular operations of the three Associations."[170] The second conference was held in response to a call from the Northampton Association[171] and the group met at the Northampton Community on August 31, 1844. The "call" had been widely published in "reformatory journals and brought together a large company"[172] with John Dwight, Mr. Dana[173] and Mr. Rykerman as delegates from Brook Farm and Adin Ballou and E. D. Draper representing Hopedale.[174] The Northampton property and physical set-up were carefully inspected and there was a long business meeting at which W. L. Garrison and Ballou discussed "Practical Christianity" and Mr. Rykerman upheld the merits of the Fourier system.[175]

Unfortunately the outcome of these meetings was not as helpful as the Northampton Community may have anticipated when it rejected Mr. Benson's offer to purchase its property, inasmuch as most of the help and advice given by their fellow associationsists seems to have been of a theoretical rather than a practical nature.[176] Mr. Benson was forced to take upon his own shoulders the responsibility of finding some means of augmenting the Association's income, and in September he purchased the patent rights to the "Woodworth Patent Planing Machine" for the sum of $500. The deed of sale stipulated that no one else could own, operate or sell the product of this machine in "North, South or West Hampton, Goshen, Hatfield, Cummington, Worthington, Williamsburg or Plainfield" except Mr. Benson acting in behalf of the Northampton Association.[177]

---

[168] *Idem.*
[169] *The Practical Christian* quoted in Ballou, *op. cit.*, p. 131-132.
[170] *Idem.*
[171] *Northampton Courier*, August 6, 1844.
[172] Ballou, *op. cit.*, p. 132.
[173] Amy L. Reed, ed. *Letters from Brook Farm, 1844-1847, by Marianne Dwight*, (Poughkeepsie, N.Y., 1928), p. 27.
[174] *The Practical Christian*, quoted in Ballou, *op. cit.*, p. 132.
[175] *Idem.*
[176] Ballou, *op. cit.*, p. 132-133.
[177] *Hampshire Country Record Book*, Vol. 121, p. 463-465.

But despite this new venture, and the report from Mr. Paine, the director of the silk-growing department, that he had realized a "net profit on capital investment in silk growing (of) 37½ percent,"[178] the Association found it necessary to raise $8,000 for running expenses by mortgaging its property to John Carter Brown, Moses and Robert Ives of Providence, in October.[179] By the end of the year a final report from the Canvassing Committee dashed whatever hopes the members had retained of the possibility of $25,000 being added to their treasury. This was particularly discouraging because it meant that the efforts of Benson, Mack and Boyle had been completely in vain since none of the subscriptions of stock were to become binding unless the full sum was raised.[180] With this news many members withdrew from the Community although paradoxically enough the Association soberly recorded their withdrawal as the reason for its failure to raise the necessary funds.[181]

Those who remained began the fourth year of the Association's existence with that same hopefulness and courage[182] which had characterized the Community's spirit from its inception, and had it not been for the crushing load of debt which confronted them they would have been more justified in this attitude than at almost any other period of the Association's existence because economic conditions were improving throughout the country, the Northampton and Springfield Railroad was nearing completion and Northampton itself was steadily developing into a larger market[183] for their products. Unfortunately the Associationists were too prone to look upon the bright side of things and they repeatedly failed to face the economic issues squarely. The point is clearly illustrated in a letter written by Mr. Hill, the Treasurer, early in 1845 in which, speaking for the Community, he says:

We are not at all discouraged or disheartened at the withdrawal of those . . . we have found . . . were not prepared for the great sacrifices (so called), the labors and trials to which we are called . . . we are aware that their withdrawal may tend to weaken confidence abroad in the success of our enterprise, and that in some instances at least they have used their influence to injure our credit. . . . There is mutually good understanding between us, and we have full confidence in each other and in our ability to transact here a profitable business. . . . In the result of past exertions and in the increasing advantages for business, we fell that we have a guaranty of future success,

[178] Northampton *Courier*, August 6, 1844.
[179] *Hampshire Country Record Book*, Vol. 105, p. 190-191.
[180] Rumsey, *op. cit.*, p. 27.
[181] Sheffeld, *op. cit.*, p. 97.
[182] *Idem.*
[183] Hardly an issue of the *Gazette* appeared without mention of these facts during the latter part of 1844, 1845 and 1846.

and unless we are cramped for means to do with, the result of another year must be triumphiantly decisive and cheering.[184]

The words of the last sentence—"unless we are cramped for means"—are almost pathetic when the Association's debt, which grew to $39,196 by mid-summer of 1845,[185] is taken into consideration together with the reports of the various departments as given at the annual meeting for that year. Only the lumber and agricultural departments were making any money. The silk manufacturing department reported that the supply of raw material was inadequate to allow them to produce at a profitable capacity; the silk growing department said that it was hopelessly behind its estimated production scale; the dyeing department had been unable to obtain any dyes; the shoemaking department was not large enough to handle or bid for large scale contracts and the cutlery department merely reported "doing nothing."[186]

Furthermore, it is evident that a certain amount of tension still existed over some of the provisions of the Constitution of 1843 as, in an attempt to bring about greater harmony among the members, several amendments to that document were made early in 1845.[187] The first of these was aimed at placating those who had objected to the distribution of net profits to all members on an absolutely equal basis, and provided for the apportionment of dividends equally in proportion to the actual amount of time devoted to working for the Association. Another amendment instituted a new system of rendering individual accounts quarterly instead of annually and a third and perhaps most important amendment provided for the election of an official to be called "The Intendant of Order."[188] The duties of this officer were "to suggest to every one connected with the Association the proper care and arrangement of the property or business of the Association and to perservere in such suggestions until they are attended to."[189] This seems to have been an attempt to give formal recognition to the system of "mutual criticism" which had been adopted by the Community,[190] and which authorized individuals to criticize the habits, conduct or personalities of their fellow members. The Northampton Association was not unique in adopting this custom as the system had been tried out at Oneida, Brook Farm and many other Communities with varying results.[191] Mr. Hill, in speaking of the plan

[184] Letter from Mr. Hill to Abner Sanger of Danvers, Massachusetts, quoted in Sheffeld, *op. cit.*
[185] Sheffeld, *op. cit.* p. 101.
[186] Rumsey, *op. cit.*, p. 27.
[187] Sheffeld, *op. cit.*, p. 98.
[188] Sheffeld, *op. cit.*, p. 98.
[189] *Idem.*
[190] Sheffeld, *op. cit.*, p. 97.
[191] Noyes, *op. cit.*, *passim.*

in after years, said that it produced among the members of the Northampton Community "a mutual familiarity with and confidence in each other, enabling them to speak plainly of errors and faults without the presence of anger."[192] But other persons connected with the group considered that the adoption of the mutual criticism system was one of the factors which contributed to the ultimate failure of the society.[193]

The absence of adequate records makes it difficult to give a comprehensive picture of the last years of the Community.[194] However, it soon becomes obvious that from 1845 onward the tide of affairs was almost unrelentingly against the interests of the Association.

When in the spring of 1845 the prospects of the silk growing industry in Massachusetts took an unexpected upward turn with the granting of a state bounty of 50¢ a pound on raw silk,[195] Mr. Paine reported that the Community had ceased to grow its own silk and was completely dependent on foreign markets for the raw material,[196] and in June the *Courier* carried an article which stated that "machinery for the manufacture of cotton is being placed in the large brick edifice at the Community in this town, heretofore occupied for making silk."[197] This change marked the beginning of the end of the Association for instead of abandoning the silk business to their more successful competitors and devoting their energies to the manufacture of cotton, the Community appropriated some of its dwindling funds for the construction of a new silk factory,[198] thus dividing the interests and energies of the members at a time when concerted effort was most necessary. This step would seem to indicate that the new administration, which had assumed control of the Community affairs in May[199] (with the election of Joseph C. Martin, formerly the head gardener,[200] to the Presidency, and Hall Judd, the storekeeper, to the Secretaryship) was no more astute than the old one had been.

After they had resigned their official positions, Mr. Mack and Mr. Benson continued to be active in the Community for some time, but they had evidently made up their minds to leave the group by July for at that time they turned over the Trusteeship to Martin and Judd.[201]

---

[192] Mr. Hill in a letter to the *Hampshire Gazette*, April 2, 1867.
[193] Sheffeld, *op. cit.*, p. 102; Rumsey, *op. cit.*, p. 28, Pressey, *op. cit.*
[194] The loss of the Association's *Record Books* is more keenly felt here than perhaps in any other section of the discussion because of the absence of adequate source material in the newspapers, etc. to augment and substantiate the information given in Sheffeld and Rumsey.
[195] Northampton *Courier*, April 22, 1845.
[196] *Idem.*
[197] Northampton *Courier*, June 10, 1845.
[198] *Idem.*, and Sheffeld, *op. cit.*, p. 99.
[199] *Hampshire County Record Book*, Vol. 109, p. 347-349.
[200] Warner, *Representative Families of Northampton* (Northampton, 1917).
[201] See note 199 above.

The strain of his many responsibilities had broken Mr. Mack's[202] health, and this together with the fact that serious disagreement had arisen over the problem of how many hours his students were to be required to spend in manual labor[203] for the group, seem to have been the primary reasons for Mr. Mack's withdrawal from the Association, which took place on September 5.[204] The family went to Woesselheft's Water Cure in Brattleboro, Vermont,[205] for a while and later moved to Belmont, Massachusetts, where Mr. Mack became active in civic affairs and was responsible for founding the town library.[206]

Mr. Benson had evidently never completely relinquished his plan for purchasing the Association's property, and after he withdrew his membership from the Community on October 1, 1845,[207] he devoted his time to organizing a stock company which would enable him to take over the cotton manufacturing business from them. He was successful in enlisting the financial support of Samuel and Joseph P. Williston and Joel Hayden,[208] and on June 29, 1846, the Bensonville Manufacturing Company bought the entire eastern section of the Community property, amounting to about one hundred and fifty acres, for $24,500 in cash and the assumption of two mortgages which amounted to an additional $16,000.[209]

This purchase liquidated a considerable portion of the Association's debt but it came too late to do any real good toward re-establishing the society on a firm foundation because membership had fallen off rapidly[210] and the departing members were demanding the return of their investments,[211] while alterations in the Constitution which provided for the investment of two-thirds of each person's dividend of the net annual income as permanent[212] stock could no more adequately fill the financial gap than the new clothing allotment of $60 a year for those over eighteen, $40 for those between eighteen and ten, and $20 for those under ten,[213] could attract enough new members to inject the needed new life into the Association. The growth of nationwide prosperity which at the outset had seemed to herald better days for the Community, in actuality mitigated against it because with the disappearance of hard times in the outside world, the rigors and sacrifices of communal life must have appeared

---

[202] Sheffeld, *op. cit.*, p. 99.
[203] *Ibid.*, p. 95 and 101.
[204] *Ibid.*, p. 99.
[205] *Idem.*
[206] Treman, *op. cit.*, p. 439.
[207] Sheffeld, *op. cit.*, p. 99.
[208] *Hampshire Gazette*, August 26, 1879.
[209] *Hampshire County Record Book*, Vol. 114, p. 154-157.
[210] Sheffeld, *op. cit.*, p. 99 and 103-105.
[211] *Ibid.*, p. 101.
[212] Sheffeld, *op. cit.*, p. 99.
[213] *Idem.*

increasingly unattractive, and many succumbed to the temptation to leave the debt ridden socialistic experiment behind them and to strike out for themselves.

The Northampton Association struggled on through the summer of 1846, reluctant to face the final reality, but at a meeting held in September there was a full discussion of the situation and it was admitted by all that there were no prospects of any more stock being subscribed.[214] The other facts were equally cheerless as the debt stood at $40,000 and they were short of operating funds despite the income from the sale of property to the Bensonville Manufacturing Company, and the $10,000 which had been obtained by mortgaging the remaining 305 acres to Amherst College.[215] The Association's Boarding School had finally been ruined by the fact that when laborers were scarce (due to the withdrawal of member) the Directors had required the older children to work during the day and receive their academic instruction in the evenings. This state of affairs angered parents both within and without the Community,[216] and of course put an end to that source of revenue. Furthermore, there was a general lack "of harmony and brotherly feeling . . . (an) unwillingness to make sacrifices, to retrench and economize . . . a lack of industry . . . (all qualities) indispensably necessary to the success of such an enterprise."[217]

The end was not far off. On November 7, 1846 the Executive Council held a long and serious meeting at the home of the Association's president, J. C. Martin, to discuss the situation. They were reluctant, in spite of the great odds, to give up the project but in view of all the circumstances there was no feasible alternative. Therefore, they proceeded to close the affairs of the Association as quickly as possible, and with the issuance of the notice that "no allowances for the subsistence of members would be made after November 1, 1846" the Community ceased to exist.[218]

The plain and practical people had been unable to sustain the dream after the dreamers had gone away. This is of course a superficial and unfair judgment upon the little group that conducted the Northampton Association in its last months because the financial foundation had been insufficient from the beginning and the policy of continual expansion coupled with the complete lack of any effort to liquidate the debt,[219] could hardly have led to anything but failure. It is true however, that as long as more than one of the original founders remained the Community

---

[214] Sheffeld, op. cit., p. 101.
[215] Hampshire County Record Book, Vol. 114, p. 269-271.
[216] Sheffeld, op. cit., p. 95 and 101.
[217] Report of meeting, September 26, 1846, quoted in Sheffeld, op. cit., p. 101.
[218] Quoted in Sheffeld, op. cit., p. 101.
[219] Noyes, op. cit., p. 156.

lived in hopes, and continued to work together to bring about "a better and purer 3tate of society."[220] It was only after Benson and Mack had withdrawn that bickering broke out and slowly, step by step, the group drifted away from the spirit of dedication to an ideal and became practical men trying merely to earn a living. All burdens are harder to bear in adversity and failure sweetens no one's temperament. The members of the Northampton Association were no exceptions to the rule; differences in religion which in the earlier days of the Community had been regarded with tolerance, if not approval, now became major obstacles[221] to communal peace; those who had looked upon dancing and card playing as unwise, now considered them one of the sources of the Association's failure.[222] The words *me* and *mine* replaced *we* and *ours* in their vocabulary, and once the ideal of brotherhood was gone the reason for their sacrifices vanished and it was time to call an end to the experiment.

It had not been a wholly wasteful and fruitless venture, but the gains to the individual were purely of an intellectual and social nature, derived from contacts with a variety of minds and ideas, and cannot be either adequately tabulated or evaluated. Some of the new ideas they championed have become commonplace or outdated today: their labor pioneering succeeded in achieving a ten hour day; women were paid the same wages as men; and although many of them reacted much as the woman who, upon being asked her opinion on a Community matter while her husband was away on a trip, replied, "My opinion has gone to the west,"[223] the women of the Northampton Association had the vote long before their fellows.

The real germ of the Northampton Association's failure lay in its lack of moderation. Its founders were filled with a burning desire to reconstruct society and had evidently forgotten the wisdom of the old adage, "make haste slowly." Their financial follies have been discussed in detail, and it seems almost unbelievable that having surveyed the course of economic suicide which they pursued, people could have been attracted to the venture as a money making proposition, and that a man such as John Carter Brown, and an institution like Amherst College, would have been willing to throw good money after bad by taking up third and fourth mortgages. There were other factors which revealed this same lack of moderation. In their desire to alleviate the sufferings of mankind the founders threw open the membership of the Community too indiscriminately and the Association suffered the consequences of the subsequent influx of social misfits. In their desire for religious toleration

[220] *Ibid.*, p. 15.
[221] *Macdonald MS, op. cit.*, p. 69.
[222] *Idem.*
[223] "Reminiscences," *op. cit.*, p. 117.

they welcomed those of all creeds or of none. In their desire for racial brotherhood they welcomed the black as warmly as the white. In their desire for universal harmony they welcomed the litterati and the illiterate, the economic prince and the pauper; and in their desire for complete equality they appointed no one leader. The result was that the Association's members were a heterogeneous group, bound by no one allegiance save the ties of humanity, and then, as now, that was not enough.

CHAPTER IV

ENTER FLORENCE

With the failure of the Association, Northampton turned its back upon the era of Emersonian transcendentalism and plunged into the stream of the technical revolution which was sweeping across America bringing with it the steel fingers and the factory mind of the machine age and its creed of progress, practicality and profit. To say that the Community's treasurer, Samuel L. Hill, had foreseen that this new voice would speak more clearly to the majority of the Associationists than the idealistic dogma of socialism which had held them in its bonds for so short a time, is of course absurd. Yet a man whose outstanding characteristics were "sagacity and deliberation"[1] must soon have realized what would be the ultimate result of the Association's economic policies, and, being endowed with a certain amount of vision or perhaps merely "Yankee shrewdness," he recognized the potentialities of the settlement and the possibilities for its profitable development in the hands of private enterprise.

Hill must have communicated something of what was in his mind to his brother-in-law, Edwin M. Eaton of Chaplin, Connecticut,[2] shortly after Benson, seeing the handwriting on the wall, had offered to buy up the Association's property early in 1844; for within the year Eaton had invested over a thousand dollars in some thirty-five acres of land near the Community.[3] By the end of 1845 he had realized more than half his capital investment through the sale of only four of those acres to men who had withdrawn from the experiment[4] but were reluctant to leave the scene of their disillusionment.

It was a wise investment in any event for Northampton was beginning to grow with an almost frantic haste. The *Hampshire Gazette* reader of 1846, like his counterpart a hundred years later, found column after column of "House Wanted" advertisements despite the fact that in 1846 more building was going on in Northampton than in any other three years put together since 1830.[5] The completion of the Springfield to Greenfield railroad had virtually deluged the town with new business and new people; the center of Northampton had long since been built up so that the newcomers, factory hands or farmers, were forced to turn to the outlying districts in order to find a place to settle.[6]

---

[1] *Hampshire Gazette*, April 2, 1867.
[2] Sheffeld, *op. cit.*, p. 208.
[3] *Hampshire County Record Book*, Vol. 102, p. 416; Vol. 105, p. 225-226.
[4] *Hampshire County Record Book*, Vol. 108, p. 9; Vol. 110, p. 455; Vol. 14, p. 377.
[5] *Hampshire Gazette*, June 2, 1846.
[6] *Ibid.*, and the Northampton *Courier* for 1846-1848.

The Bensonville Manufacturing Company had laid out a neat "village" of 26 building lots near its factory in an effort to solve the housing problem of its operatives and anyone else who cared to buy;[7] and with the closing of the Association the real estate boom spread to Eaton's Village as Hill's brother-in-law called his property which lay just west of the Cotton Factory lands.[8] Ex-Associationists immediately bought up plots in both developments either for cash or on credit,[9] and began the process of readjustment to life in the outside world. Some of them like Austin Ross, who purchased the Community farm and began the settlement's first commercial milk business,[10] devoted themselves to independent agriculture; while others continued to work in the silk mill which Mr. Hill kept in operation,[11] or sought employment in the nearby cotton mills[12] which were advertising for: "Experienced weavers and others to work . . . (for) as good wages as at the best mills in the country."[13]

The trustees of the Association, Martin, Hill and Judd, in their struggle to dissolve the Community's debts and liabilities made an attempt to capitalize on this sudden market for land, and were successful in selling off several sections of the estate[14] which they advertized as:

> Pleasantly and conveniently situated for the residence of persons engaged in business at Bensonville, Hopeville, and the Northampton Association . . . (where) Tenements (were) much needed for the accommodation of the increased an (sic) increasing manufacturing and mercantile business.[15]

The sale of a partial interest in the Woodworth Patent Planing Machine, which Benson had so hopefully purchased in 1844, also brought in ready cash and by 1848 they had realized something over fifteen thousand dollars.[16] At this juncture Martin and Judd accepted ten thousand dollars for their interest in the remaining, and by far the most valuable section of the property, which strangely enough—for it contained the factory, machine shops, store and oil mill[17]—had never been offered for public sale. The man who purchased the last of the Association's holdings was its erstwhile Treasurer, Samuel L. Hill.

---

[7] *Hampshire County Record Book,* Vol. 115, p. 360.
[8] *Ibid.,* Vol. 116, p. 360.
[9] *Ibid.,* Vol. 114, p. 405-406; Vol. 116, p. 197, 207, 376-377; Vol. 117, p. 21-22, 28-29.
[10] *Hampshire Gazette,* April 2, 1867.
[11] Sheffeld, *op. cit.,* p. 208.
[12] *Hampshire Gazette,* April 2, 1867.
[13] *Ibid.,* May 11, 1847.
[14] *Hampshire County Record Book,* Vol. 121, p. 142-143; Vol. 124, p. 417, 418, 434-435; Vol. 129, p. 314-315.
[15] *Hampshire Gazette,* March 16, 1847.
[16] *Hampshire County Record Book,* Vol. 121, p. 463-465; see also note 14 above.
[17] *Ibid.,* Vol. 125, p. 172-173.

During the first years of the transition from Community to village Hill had acted as his brother-in-law's agent but by 1849 he had absorbed virtually all of Eaton's remaining interest in the unsold property in Eaton's village and was conducting a brisk real estate business[18] of his own. Many of his customers had been his fellow associationists and towards them he seems to have exercised a policy of paternalistic leniency, granting small loans and extending credit to enable them to establish homes.[19]

Although George Benson had resigned from the Association some time before the venture was given up, he too retained a very real interest in the welfare of the communists, especially the negro members. He was supported in this by his partners in the cotton business, and it became a policy of the Bensonville Manufacturing Company to give "employment to . . . colored brethren . . . and they were . . . put on a par with other races and nationalities in that mill."[20] In addition to this general interest, Benson took upon himself the responsibility of providing for Sojourner Truth who, no longer a young woman, was crushed and bewildered by the closing of the Association which she had come to regard as her permanent home.[21] Basil Dorsey, a fugitive slave who had come to the Community in 1844, was another of Benson's protégees, and being young and strong he was put in charge of all the teaming for the cotton factory. Evidently Dorsey had a pleasing personality for he so thoroughly won the respect and affection of the townspeople that in 1850 they got together and made up a purse which, with the addition of fifty dollars of his own savings, made it possible to purchase his freedom from his old master. This enabled Dorsey to carry merchandise to Boston and other nearby cities without fear of being captured by slavehunters, and materially increased his earnings.[22]

In addition to such practical applications of his firm belief in universal brotherhood, Benson also kept up an active participation in the religious reform movement and in 1848 presided over a two day session of the Anti-Sabbath Convention in Boston.[23] Whether these interests made so heavy a demand upon his time and finances that he was unable to give the necessary attention to his business commitments can only be conjectured, but sometime[24] during 1850 it became obvious that Benson's

[18] *Ibid.*, see *Grantee* and *Grantor Index* under S. L. Hill, in the Northampton *Registry of Deeds;* references are too numerous to cite here.
[19] Sheffeld, *op. cit.*, p. 208.
[20] *Hampshire Gazette*, August 26, 1879.
[21] *Narrative of Sojourner Truth, op. cit.*, p. 121.
[22] *Hampshire Gazette*, May 20, 1850; also April 2, 1867.
[23] Garrison, *op. cit.*, Vol. 3, p. 221, 226.
[24] There is no record of this failure among the files of the *Northampton Registry of Probate.* It is the opinion of that office that the case either came under the jurisdiction of the United States Court or was settled out of court. Sheffeld and the *Hampshire Gazette* give no definite dates.

financial affairs were hopelessly involved and he was forced to withdraw from the cotton manufacturing business.[25] After a short stay in Williamsburg, Mr. Benson moved to Wakarusa township, Kansas, where he continued his interest in the reform and abolition movements[26] and was active in the legislature.[27]

Benson's failure did not materially effect the industrial development of the district because his partners, Samuel and J. P. Williston, and Joel Hayden, continued the business under the firm name of the Greenville Manufacturing Company,[28] but the name of the settlement soon changed by tacit popular consent from Bensonville to Greenville.[29]

Samuel L. Hill had given Benson considerable material support and the latter's failure made Hill responsible for the notes which he had endorsed.[30] In order to meet the immediate pressure of the demands of Benson's creditors, Hill placed two mortgages (one for $4,000 to the recently established Smith Charities,[31] and the other for $1,000 to the Northampton Institution for Savings[32]) on his silk mill property which included, in addition to the factory, a dye house, saw mill, steam engine, water wheel, oil mill, wood house, store and blacksmith shop.[33] He also was able to raise some $3291 through the sale of lots in Eaton's Village,[34] and it is interesting to note that many of the purchasers were ex-Associationists, and two of them, Basil Dorsey[35] and "Isabella Vanwagner sometimes called Sojourner Truth,"[36] were former protégees of Mr. Benson's.

Despite the burden imposed on him by such heavy indebtedness, Hill continued his interest in building up the region as a manufacturing center; and, having secured the financial support of Mr. Samuel L. Hinckley, a wealthy Northampton resident, he bought the silk factory of the Northampton Association's former competitor Arthur Valentine.[37] By August of 1851 the Nonotuck Steam Silk Mill, "Mr. S. L. Hill agent, S. L. Hinckley owner . . . located on the plain a little north of Green-

---

[25] Sheffeld, *op. cit.*, p. 108-109; *Hampshire Gazette*, April 2, 1867.
[26] Undated letter from Mr. Benson to Mrs. Garrison in *Garrison Collection*.
[27] *Hampshire Gazette*, August 26, 1879.
[28] *Ibid.*, April 2, 1867; also *Business Directory, op. cit.*, p. 96.
[29] *Hampshire Gazette*, April 2, 1867; also all references to the section after 1850.
[30] Sheffeld, *op. cit.*, p. 108-109. No specific sum is mentioned but Sheffeld says Hill was completely ruined by Benson's failure-in observation which does not seem to be substantiated by the records in the *Registry of Deeds*, but Mr. Sheffeld may have had access to other records unavailable to this author.
[31] *Hampshire County Record Book*, Vol. 151, p. 111.
[32] *Ibid.*, Vol. 141, p. 232-233.
[33] *Hampshire County Record Book*, Vol. 151, p. 168-169.
[34] *Ibid.*, Vol. 132, p. 100; Vol. 133, p. 431, 468-469, 225; Vol. 134, p. 201; Vol. 135, p. 167; Vol. 141, p. 282-283; 374-375; Vol. 151, p. 162-163.
[35] *Ibid.*, Vol. 142, p. 489-490.
[36] *Ibid.*, Vol. 133, p. 106.
[37] *Hampshire Gazette*, April 2, 1867; Sheffeld, *op. cit.*, p. 208-209.

ville (was producing) 5,000 pounds of silk a year (and employing) 20 operatives."[38]

Although predominently an industrial village, Greenville was the home of the first "Water Cure" in Northampton.[39] Hydropathy, or the water cure system, had come into vogue in America in the early forties and, in addition to a "course of baths," the patients were required to live simple, healthful lives preferably in secluded country retreats. The territory around the Northampton Association was particularly suitable for a hydropathy establishment due to the convenient and abundant supply

DR. MUNDE'S WATER CURE
Redrawn by C. L. Gethman from a print in Sheffeld's
History of Florence.

of water from the Mill River, and it was still relatively isolated. During the last year of the Association's life "Dr." David Ruggles, the blind negro whom the Community had befriended, succeeded in raising $2,000 in Northampton[40] and began a water cure near the grounds. His small establishment could treat only forty persons at a time and the rates were $5.50 a week for double and $8.50 for single rooms, with washing extra and every patient had to supply his own blankets and linen.[41] Despite the relatively Spartan character of the retreat, Ruggles prospered during the first year but by 1847 Mr. Samuel Whitmarsh (the original founder of the Northampton Silk Company) had another water cure in operation on Round Hill, which because of its more convenient location and superior

[38] *Hampshire Gazette*, August 5, 1851.
[39] *Ibid.*, August 4, 1846.
[40] *Hampshire Gazette*, August 4, 1846.
[41] *Ibid.*, May 1, 1847.

accommodations, as well as the attendance of two accredited physicians,[42] must have been more attractive to the wealthy visitors some five thousand of whom came every season to admire the beautiful homes and fine views of New England's most popular summer resort.[43]

The following year (1848) saw the opening of Dr. E. E. Dennison's Springdale Water Cure in an old hotel "about a mile and a half west of the business center"[44] of Northampton. Such competition proved disastrous for Ruggles' modest establishment, and despite the fact that Mr. Hill gave him financial assistance on at least two occasions,[45] and the local papers carried frequent and glowing testironials of his skill, only his death[46] on December 16, 1849 forestalled bankruptcy.[47] This unhappy precedent did not prevent Dr. Charles Munde from purchasing the property at public auction in 1850. With funds loaned by S. L. Hill and Charles Smith, the trustee's of the Ruggles estate,[48] Munde repaired the buildings and, by catering almost exclusively to Southerners, soon had a prosperous and thriving business.[49]

In the seven years that followed the closing of the Northampton Association of Education and Industry the little settlement in Broughton's Meadows changed from a quiet, isolated, community to a growing manufacturing village; and if the change brought substantial material gains it also brought cultural, intellectual and spiritual losses. The weekly lyceums, the lectures, the book clubs and discussion groups vanished with the Association. The seventy-four children of Warner School District[50] no longer learned their lessons from progressive teachers in the fields and along the banks of Mill River, but were taught their AB BA's in a more conventional, if less enlightened, manner by a country schoolmaster[51] in a one-room brick school house which the town of Northampton erected on land granted to it for that purpose by S. L. Hill and J. P. Williston.[52] Religious education suffered even more severe a blow, as the dissolution of the Association brought an end to organized church services in the district for almost fifteen years.[53]

There were other changes too. In 1850 Mr. Hill formed a partnership with Isaac S. Parsons, and the old Community Store, which he had con-

[42] *Ibid.*, October 26, 1847.
[43] Mrs. David Lee Childs in the Northampton *Courier*, November 30, 1841.
[44] *Business Directory, op. cit.*, p. 99.
[45] *Hampshire County Record Book*, Vol. 127, p. 301-302.
[46] *Business Directory, op. cit.*, p. 100.
[47] *Hampshire County Record Book*, Vol. 101, p. 324-329.
[48] *Business Directory, op. cit.*, p. 100.
[49] Paul F. Munde, "The Munde Water Cure" in Sheffeld, *op. cit.*, p. 190-193.
[50] *Hampshire Gazette*, May 22, 1849.
[51] *The Warner District School Record Book*, quoted in Sheffeld, *op. cit.*, p. 152.
[52] *Hampshire County Record Book*, Vol. 130, p. 340.
[53] "Religious History of Florence" in Sheffeld, *op. cit.*, p. 137-150.

tinued to operate alone after the failure of the Association, became the firm of I. S. Parsons & Co.;[54] while W. A. Godfrey opened up a store in the cotton factory's old boarding house that same year.[55] Although farms and factories existed side by side at Greenville in 1852, the factories were gradually absorbing more and more of the working population and producing more and more of its total consumer goods. The Nonotuck Steam Silk Mill was expanding its business, plans were being laid for the construction of a button and daguerreotype factory[56] and with the steady advance of the industrial revolution, the settlement ceased to be merely a factory village under the paternalistic domination of mill owners as the cognomen Greenville implied. The people were no longer dependent upon Northampton for the majority of commodities they used in daily living, and in an attempt to assert their independence they petitioned the United States Government for a post office of their own.[57] In the years immediately following the close of the Association all mail addressed to residents of Bensonville or Greenville had been placed in Mr. Hill's box at the Northampton post office. However, the expanding population of the district was rapidly rendering this situation untenable.[58] Understandably enough Northampton was reluctant to lose the trade which the old arrangement had brought into town and hotly contested the petition,[59] but on December 28, 1852, they lost the fight and the new post office was installed in I. S. Parson's store.[60] While the struggle over the post office was still going on the residents of Greenville met together and, at the suggestion of Messers. Hill, Munde and Parsons, formally voted to adopt a new name for their community,[61] a name which, while it carried a memory of the settlement's humble origin, might presage a golden future. In the *Hampshire Gazette* for February 24, 1852 appeared this notice:

The citizens of "Bensonville or Greenville" dissatisfied with either of the names mentioned have adopted the name of Florence for their village. Inasmuch as the business of the village is dependent, in no small degree upon the silk manufacture, the name is not inappropriate.[62]

[54] *Hampshire Gazette*, April 12, 1867.
[55] *Idem.*
[56] Agnes Hannay, "A Chronicle of Industry on the Mill River" in *Smith College Studies in History*, Vol. XXI, Nos. 1-4, (October 1935—July, 1936), p. 78.
[57] *Hampshire Gazette*, April 2, 1867.
[58] Sheffeld, *op. cit.*, p. 108.
[59] *Hampshire Gazette*, April 2, 1867.
[60] Sheffeld, *op. cit.*, p. 108.
[61] *Ibid.*, p. 107.
[62] *Hampshire Gazette*, February 24, 1852.

BIBLIOGRAPHY

PRIMARY SOURCES

Books and Pamphlets

Ballau, Adin, *The Hopedale Community*, Lowell, 1897.

Bigelow, John P., *Statistical Tables: Exhibiting the Conditions and Products of Certain Branches of Industry in Massachusetts for year ending April 1, 1837*, Boston, 1838.

Brisbane, Arnold, *The Social Destiny of Man*, Philadelphia, 1840.

Codman, John T., *Brook Farm, Historic & Personal Memoirs*, Boston, 1894.

DeBow, J. E. B., *Statistical View of United States, Compendium of Seventh Census*, Washington, 1854.

First Report of New England Silk Convention, Northampton, 1842.

Gide, Charles, ed., *Selections from the works of Fourier*, London, 1901.

Historical Register and General Directory of Northampton, Northampton, 1875.

Holland, J. G., *History of Western Massachusetts*, Springfield, 1855.

McLaren, Donald C., *Boa Constrictor or Fourier Association Self-Exposed as to its Principles and Aims*, Rochester, 1844.

Narrative of Sojourner Truth, Boston, 1850.

Northampton Business Directory, Northampton, 1861.

Noyes, John Humphrey, *History of American Socialism*, Philadelphia, 1870.

Owen, Robert, *New View of Society and other Writings*, New York, 1927.

Sheffeld, Charles A., ed., *The History of Florence, Massachusetts*, Florence, 1895.

Trumbull, J. R., *History of Northampton, Massachusetts, from its settlement in 1654*, Northampton, 1898.

Whitmarsh, Samuel, *Eight Years' Experience and Observation in Culture of Mulberry tree and in Care of Silk Worm*, Northampton, 1839.

Letters and Journals

Crane, Mrs. Bathsheba H., *Life, Letters and Wayside Gleanings for the Folks at Home*, Boston, 1880.

Curti, Merle, *The Learned Blacksmith*, New York, 1937.

Dwight, Marianne, *Letters from Brook Farm, 1844-1847*, Poughkeepsie, 1928.

William Lloyd Garrison, 1805-1879, The story of his life told by his children, 3 vol., New York, 1885.

Judd, Sylvester, *Memorabilia*, edited by Arethusa Hall, Northampton, 1882.

Lesley, Susan I., *Recollections of My Mother, Mrs. Anne Jean Lyman of Northampton*, Boston, 1899.

Newspapers

The Hampshire Gazette, Northampton, 1825-1856.

The Northampton Courier, Northampton, 1837-1852.

Periodicals

Hawthorne, Manning, "Hawthorne and Utopian Socialism," *New England Quarterly*, v. 12, 1939.

Lane, Charles, "Brook Farm," *Dial*, v. IV, Boston, 1844.

McMaster, J. A., "Society Theories," *American Whig Review*, v. VII, New York, 1848.

Niles Weekly Register, v. XXIV-LXX, Baltimore, 1828-1846.

Peabody, E. P., "Fourierism," *Dial*, v. IV, Boston, 1844.

Smart, George K., "Fourierism in Northampton: Two Documents," *New England Quarterly*, v. 12, 1939.

Government Publications

Register of Debates in Congress, v. VI, part II, Washington, 1830.

Manuscripts

Judd, Sylvester, *Day Book*, Northampton, 1829-1834.

Letters of Wm. Adam, George Benson, S. L. Hill and David Mack, 1838-1867, in the Garrison Collection, Boston Public Library.

Macdonald, A. J., *A History of American Communities*, Yale University Library, New Haven, Connecticut.

Record of Town Meetings, Northampton, 1830-1856.

Registry of Deeds Record Books, Northampton, 1828-1856.

SECONDARY SOURCES

Books and Pamphlets

Arvin, Newton, *Hawthorne*, Boston, 1929.

Beard, Charles A., and Mary R., *Rise of American Civilization*, v. 1, New York, 1943.

Bidwell, P. W., and Falconer, J. I., *History of Agriculture in Northern United States: 1620-1860*, Washington, 1925.

Brockett, L. P., *The Silk Industry in America*, np., 1876.

Calverton, Victor Francis, *Where Angels Dared to Tread*, New York, 1941.

Cooke, George Willis, *Unitarianism in America*, Boston, 1902.

Faulkner, Harold U., *American Economic History*, New York, 1929.

————, *American Political and Social History*, New York, 1940.

Fish, C. R., *The Rise of the Common Man*, (*History of American Life Series*) New York, 1939.

Gere, Henry S., *Reminiscences of Old Northampton*, Northampton, 1902.

Haraszti, Zoltan, *The Idyll of Brook Farm*, Boston, 1937.

Hart, A. B., *Slavery and Abolition, a History*, (*American Nation Series*, v. 16), New York, 1906.

Hillquit, Morris, *History of Socialism in the United States*, New York, 1906.

Hinds, William A., *American Communities and Co-operative Colonies*, Chicago, 1908.

Jones, L., *The Life, Times and Labours of Robert Owen*, London, 1890.

Laidler, Harry W., *A History of Socialist Thought*, New York, 1827.

————, *Social-economic movements*, New York, 1946.

Lichtenberger, André, *Le Socialisme Utopique*, Paris, 1898.

McMaster, J. B., *A History of the People of the United States*, v. 7, New York, 1910.

Matsui, Schichiro, *The History of the Silk Industry in the United States*, New York, 1930.

Nordhoff, Charles, *Communistic Societies of the United States, from personal visit and observation*, New York, 1875.

Sotheran, Charles, *Horace Greeley and other pioneers of American socialism*, New York, 1915.

Swift, Lindsay, *Brook Farm*, New York, 1908.

Treman, E. M., and Poole, M. E., *The History of the Treman, Tremaine, Truman Family in America*, Ithaca, New York, 1901.

Turner, F. J., *The United States, 1830-1850*, New York, 1935.

Weigle, L. A., *American Idealism, (Pageant of America Series*, v. 10), New Haven, 1928.

Wyckoff, W. C., *Report on Silk Manufacturing Industry of United States*, Washington, 1885.

Periodicals and Encyclopedias

Douglas, D. W., and Lumpkin, K., "Communistic Settlements," *Encyclopedia of the Social Sciences*, v. 2, New York, 1937.

Frothingham, O. B., "Some Phases of Idealism in New England," *Atlantic Monthly*, v. 52, Boston, 1883.

"George Ripley and the Brook Farm Association," *Living Age*, v. 67, Boston, 1860.

Hannay, Agnes, "A Chronicle of Industry on the Mill River," *Smith College Studies in History*, v. 21, Northampton, 1936.

Mason, Edward S., "Fourier and Fourierism," *Encyclopedia of the Social Sciences*, v. 6, New York, 1937.

Pressey, J. B., "Northampton Community," *Country, Time, and Tide*, v. 4, Palmyra, New York, 1903.

Rumsey, Olive, "The Northampton Association of Education and Industry," *New England Magazine*, v. 12, Boston, 1895.

"Silk," *The Encyclopedia Americana*, v. 25, New York, 1944.

Manuscripts

Bestor, Arthur E., Jr., *American Phalanxes, a Study of Fourieristic Socialism in the United States*, 2 v., New Haven, 1928.

Cobb, Elizabeth, *Intellectual History of Northampton in the 1840's*, Smith College, 1932.

Hooper, Rev. J. Harry, *The Beginnings of Florence and Northampton*, Florence, 1825.

Houghton, Ruth, *The Silk Industry in Northampton*, Smith College, 1929.

Kneeland, Frederick N., *Reminiscences of Old Northampton*, Forbes Library, Northampton.

Lathrop, Bessie S., *Daniel Stebbins and the Silk Industry in Northampton*, Forbes Library, Northampton.

APPENDICES

APPENDIX A
PRELIMINARY CIRCULAR.*

When existing institutions are found inadequate to promote the further progress of society, it becomes the duty of those who perceive the necessity of reform, to associate together upon principles, in their opinion, the best calculated to fulfill the designs of God in placing man in this life. Among those designs are believed to be the progressive culture and high development of all the powers and faculties of our nature; the union of spiritual, intellectual, and practical attainments; the equality of rights and rank for all, except that those stations and pursuits should be regarded as most honorable which promote self-conquest and the most expansive philanthropy; and the practical recognition of the responsibility of every individual to God alone in all his pursuits. These designs of God demand the co-operation of man as an essential condition, but existing institutions of education and business do not afford it, inasmuch as they fail to provide for the full development of the faculties of any class or individual; recognize invidious distinctions, assigning the highest rank for other reasons than moral worth; establish separate and conflicting action for various kinds and degrees of culture, skill, and labor; forbid such freedom of thinking and acting as is required by personal accountability; sever intellectual culture from action in such a manner as to make it barren and even subversive of moral principle; and separate labor from speculative pursuits so as to make it drudgery, thus causing the degradation of a necessary means of education, health, and happiness. The following Articles of Association are proposed, as a means of reducing to practice the foregoing principles: —

ARTICLE I. The name and style of this association shall be The Northampton Association of Education and Industry.

ART. II. The management of the affairs and undertakings of this Association shall be conducted by two distinct companies: 1st, a Stock Company; 2d, an Industrial Association.

ART. III. The Stock Company shall be first formed by obtaining a subscription of $100,000. to be paid in money or some equivalent at the option of the Stock Directors. As soon as $50,000 are secured by binding subscriptions, $30,000 of which, at least, shall be paid by the first of April next, the company shall be organized by choosing a President, Secretary and Treasurer, who together shall as Trustees, hold all the property of the Association in trust until their successors shall be appointed by the Company.

ART. IV. The President and Secretary shall sign all contracts and papers binding the Company, and the Treasurer shall give security to the satisfaction of the Company for the safe keeping of its money and papers; but the Trustees shall not have power to buy or sell, as agents of the Company, on credit.

ART. V The Secretary shall keep a book in which copies of all the shares shall be entered, with the names of their owners, and all interest and dividends due thereon. No transfer of stock shall be valid unless indorsed by the President and Secretary; and a copy of every transfer shall be entered on the Secretary's book. But no transfer shall be authorized for any person indebted to the Association until security be given for the payment of his debt.

ART. VI. The Secretary shall keep account of all the property, contracts and obligations of the Company, and of the obligations and money transactions of each member with the Company; and at suitable times those accounts may be inspected by any member of the Company.

ART. VII. The Secretary shall make annually an inventory of all the property of the Association, an adjusted statement of its pecuniary conditions, and a full settlement of its transactions with other parties and with each member of the Company; so that at the beginning of each year new accounts may be opened.

ART. VIII. New stock may be raised at any time and to any amount determined by a vote of two-thirds of the stockholders.

---

*Reprinted from Charles A. Sheffeld, ed., *The History of Florence, Massachusetts* (Florence, Mass.: published by the editor, 1895), pp. 69-73.

ART. IX. Shares shall be for $100 each, negotiable under the restrictions of the fifth Article, and shall be entitled to annual interest not exceeding six per cent; but interest shall not be payable under four years, when the annual interest and the interest for the four years then due may be paid, or the arrears may be equally divided between the next four years, at the option of the Company.

ART. X. Interest or dividends of profits may be paid in stock or in cash, at the option of the stockholder; but the Company shall not be obliged to pay cash, unless previous notice be given to the Secretary thirty days before the payment becomes due.

ART. XI. In settling with individual members, each shall be charged with rent of apartments furnished by the Stock Company at a reasonable rate, and with supplies furnished by the Association at cost.

ART. XII. In stock transactions, every share shall be entitled to one vote, provided that no one proprietor shall be entitled to more than ten votes. In the absence of stockholders, their shares may be represented by proxies.

ART XIII. Every certificate of stock shall contain a condition providing that shares owned by persons not members of the Industrial Association may be bought in, upon payment of principal and interest, by members of the Association, when notice of such intention shall be given thirty days before the annual interest becomes due.

ART. XIV. In making the annual statement, the disbursements shall be made in the following order: 1st, expenses of stock transactions and management, including labor; 2d, expenses of supporting members of the Industrial Association unable to earn a support, the property of such members in the stock account being first applied as far as it will go; 3d, six per cent. on all stock actually paid in. The balance shall be divided among the members of the Industrial Association in proportion to their several services in labor and talent or skill, to be estimated by the books and reports of the Leaders of Divisions and Subdivisions, two-thirds of said balance being awarded to labor, and one-third to skill.

ART. XV. The Stock Directors shall determine in what manner their funds shall be invested, and shall make such appropriations for carrying on the different branches of business as they shall judge best, those branches being most favored that are necessary and less attractive. They may always attend the meetings of the Board of Directors of the Industrial Association and give their advice, but shall not be allowed to vote.

ART. XVI. Any member expelled or choosing to withdraw, shall receive all that is due on the stock account, at the next annual settlement, if he give ninety days' previous notice, and before receiving the same shall sign a full discharge of all claims against the Company or the Association.

ART. XVII. The Stock Company when duly organized shall elect twenty families to commence the Industrial Association. Those twenty families, together with such families and individuals as shall be admitted members, shall elect all subsequent members, and may expel an unworthy member.

ART. XVIII. The Industrial Association shall be organized by choosing a Director for each branch of employment established by the Association, with the advice of the Stock Trustees. Such Directors shall form a Board, who shall see that suitable employment for all the members shall always be provided; shall be arbitrators to settle all difficulties between the Divisions or Subdivisions, or between individuals, at the expense of the party by them decided to be in the wrong, such expense being only the value of time, rooms, etc., caused by the arbitration; and shall fix the rate of compensation for the various employments and ages, awarding higher compensation to the most necessary and disagreeable rather than to the most productive. They shall manage the purchase of materials and goods for the Association and for individuals, and the sale of articles produced or manufactured by the Association, but they shall never buy or sell on credit.

ART. XIX. Each branch of employment shall be prosecuted by such as choose it, who shall form a class, consisting of as many Divisions as the Directors shall determine; each Division shall choose a Leader who shall determine the number of subdivisions; and each Subdivision shall choose its Leader, who shall keep an account of the labor and skill of each member of his Subdivision at each time of meeting, and shall report the progress of his undertaking to the Board of Directors annually and as often as necessary. All the leaders of Subdivisions shall form a Committee for consultation concerning the best ways and means of managing the business of their Division.

ART. XX. Each Subdivision shall determine the manner in which their employment shall be performed, shall assign different portions to individuals according to their qualifications, and shall admit new members, who may be qualified, upon their application.

ART. XXI. Each Subdivision shall, as far as practicable, consist of different sexes and ages, so that the heavier parts may be performed by the stronger; the lighter, by the more delicate individuals.

ART. XXII. No charge shall be made to any member of the Association or his family for religious or other instruction, for medical attendance or nursing by members of the Association, or for the use of baths, public rooms, or whatever is provided for the general use and benefit, unless used for some private or particular purpose.

ART. XXIII. Every man, woman, and child above the age of five years shall have a separate account with the Association, and shall have a separate and distinct interest. The expenses and the compensation of children shall be so arranged that the profits of their industry shall refund the cost of their support by the time they become admissible as members of the Association.

ART. XXIV. This Association and any of its Boards or Committees may establish such By-laws not inconsistent with the spirit and intention of this Declaration and of these Articles, as they may think proper, from time to time.

ART. XXV. Any of these articles may be altered at a regular meeting of the Association, by a majority of two-thirds of the members; provided notice of the proposed alteration shall be given in the manner to be prescribed in the By-laws.

BROUGHTON MEADOWS, NORTHAMPTON, February 15, 1842.

At a meeting of the owners of the property known as the Northampton Silk Factory Estate, held this 15th day of February, 1842, Joseph Conant was voted President, and William Adam, Secretary. Whereupon, it was unanimously

Resolved, That, approving of the principles and objects developed in the preceding Declaration and Articles of Association, we, the owners of the aforesaid Estate, consisting of about four hundred and twenty acres of land; six dwelling houses; a large brick factory, nearly new, four stories high, measuring one hundred and twenty by forty feet, with water-wheel, gear, and shafting fit for operation, and situated on a durable stream of water called Mill River, having from twenty-seven to twenty-nine feet fall; a dye-house, with necessary apparatus; a wooden building about thirty feet square, formerly used for manufacturing purposes, with water-wheel, in good condition; a saw-mill; a Raymond's shingle mill, with patent right secured for the town of Northampton, capable of cutting ten thousand shingles per hour; a planing machine for planing and jointing boards, planks, and timber; turning lathes, circular saws, &c., &c., together with machinery in the factory adapted to the manufacture of silk, and sundry other articles of personal property; also a lot of pine timber, containing about fifty acres, about a mile and a half from the saw-mill: — the whole estimated to be worth about thirty thousand dollars, — are willing and ready to place it at the disposal of the projected Northampton Association of Education and Industry, at a fair valuation, whenever fifty thousand dollars of stock shall be subscribed, and thirty thousand dollars paid up, as specified in the Articles already referred to.

(Signed)

W. Adam,   Joseph Conant,

  Secretary.   *President.*

In conformity to the preceding Declaration of Sentiments and Articles of Association, and in consideration of the foregoing proceedings of the proprietors of the Northampton Silk Company Estate, We, the undersigned, do severally subscribe to the Stock Company therein set forth the number of shares set against our names, the amount of which we promise to pay as herein specified to the Treasurer of said Company; the said Stock property to be forever holden and managed in all respects according to the principles and provisions of the aforesaid Declaration and Articles.

APPENDIX B*

NORTHAMPTON ASSOCIATION OF EDUCATION AND INDUSTRY

It is impossible to survey the present condition of the world, the institutions of society, the general character of mankind, and their prevailing pursuits and tendencies, without perceiving the great evils that afflict humanity, and recognizing many of them as the direct consequences of existing social arrangements.

Life is with some a mere round of frivolous occupations or vicious enjoyments; with most a hard struggle for the bare means of subsistence. The former are exempted from productive labor while they enjoy its fruits; upon the latter it is imposed as a task with unreasonable severity and with inadequate compensation. The one class is tempted to self-indulgence, pride and oppression: the other is debased by ignorance and crime, by the conflict of passions and interests, by moral pollution, and by positive want and starvation.

The governments of the world are systematically warlike in their constitution and spirit, in the measures they adopt, and in the means they employ to establish and support their power to redress their real and alleged grievances, without regard to truth, justice, or humanity, and political parties are notoriously and characteristically destitute of all principle except the love of place and the emoluments which it bestows, without consideration for the true advancement of society.

Religion, whose essence is perfect spiritual liberty and universal knowledge, is prostituted into a device for tyrannizing over the minds of men by arraying them into hostile sects, by substituting audible and visible forms for the inward power of truth and goodness, and by rendering the superstitious fear and irresponsible dicatation of men paramount to the veneration and authority that belong only to God.

For these evils, viz. extreme ignorance and poverty in immediate juxtaposition with the most insolent licentiousness; adverse and contending interests; war, slavery, party-corruption, and selfishness; sectarian exclusiveness and spiritual tyranny, society as at present constituted affords no remedy. On the contrary, it has sprung out of these evils, is maintained by them, and has a direct tendency to re-produce them in a constantly increasing progression; and the human mind is driven to the conclusion either that the Infinitely Wise and Benevolent Creator of the world designed to produce a state of things subversive of moral goodness and destructive to human happiness, which is a contradiction in terms; or that man, necessarily imperfect and therefore liable to err, has mistaken his path by neglecting the light which Nature and Religion were intended to³ [afford] for the attainment of Truth and Righteousness, Purity and Freedom.

No believer in God can doubt that it is not He who has failed in his purpose, but man who has wandered from his true course, and after the perception of this truth and of the insufficiency of existing institutions to correct the manifold evils of society and promote its further progress, it is the duty of all to endeavor, to discover and adopt purer and more salutary principles, and to apply them individually and collectively to the regulation of their conduct in life. The vices of the present forms and practices of civilization are so gross and palpable that no apology is required for the honest attempt to escape from them, even although it should not be accompanied with the pretence of peculiar wisdom and virtue and should not be followed by the complete success which is both desirable and attainable. The following principles indicating dangers to be avoided, duties to be performed, and rights to be maintained, are adopted as a bond of union and basis of co-operation.

---

*Reset from the facsimile in the first edition of *From Utopia to Florence*. That facsimile was a photostat copy of the pages of the Macdonald Ms. containing an account of the Northampton Association of Education and Industry together with the Constitutions of that Society for the years 1842 and 1843. This is the only known copy of the Constitution of 1843. The original document, which consists of newspaper clippings, articles and testimonials about this and other communities, is in the possession of the Yale University Library.

I. Productive labor is the duty of every human being, and every laborer has the exclusive right of enjoying and disposing of the fruits of his labor.

II. The opportunity of self-improvement in all knowledge is the right of every human being.

III. It is the right of every human being to express the dictates of his conscience on religious and all other subjects and to worship God under any form or in any manner agreeable to his convictions of duty, not interfering with equal rights of others.

IV. Fair argument is the only legitimate means of controlling the opinions or belief of another, and no praise or blame, no merit or demerit, no reward or punishment, ought to be awarded for any opinions or belief, for which every human being is responsible to God alone.

V. The rights of all are equal without distinction of sex, color or condition, sect or religion.

VI. The family relation, the relation between husband and wife and between parents and children, has its foundation and support in the laws of Nature and the will of God, in the affections of the heart and the dictates of the understanding. Other and wider relations may be formed for the purposes of social improvement, but none that are inconsistent with this which is sacred and permanent, the root and foundation of all human excellence and hapiness.

VII. The combination of individuals and families is an evil or good according to the objects to which it is directed. To combine for the purpose of inflicting an injury is evil: to combine for the purpose of protecting from injury or conferring a benefit is good. To combine for the purposes of war, agression, conquest, tyranny, and enslavement is evil: to combine for the purpose of living in peace and amity towards all, and in the exercise of mutual benevolence and friendly offices is good. To combine for the purpose of spreading speculative doctrines and ceremonial observances, forms of religious worship and discipline, is injurious to the welfare of mankind, because belief is constantly changing in every individual mind according to the fresh accessions of light and knowledge which it receives, and because a fixed profession is not and cannot be the true index of a varying belief, and because such combinations therefore necessarily tend to produce habits of insincerity, to restrain freedom of thought and expression on the most momentous subjects, to cause the outward show of religion to take the place of its practical and spiritual influences, and to afford an instrument to priests and tyrants to enslave the mind and the body. On the other hand, to combine for the purpose of counteracting, within a greater or less sphere, the causes which have produced ignorance and vice, oppression and crime, bigotry, fanaticism, and intolerance; of raising labor to its true dignity and giving to it its just rewards; of economizing labor and increasing its productiveness by means of machinery, of co-operation, and of a wise division of the departments of industry; of securing the full enjoyment of liberty in thought, in word, and in action; and of promoting the progressive culture and full development of all the capacities of human nature by the union of spiritual, intellectual, and practical attainments, is conducive to the happiness and improvement of the world, promotes the cause of freedom, of truth, and of goodness, and according to their means and opportunities is the right, the duty, and the interest of all.

Such are the principles and objects of the Northampton Association of Education and Industry, and it is in the full and distinct recognition of their truth and obligation and with the view of applying them in practice that the following regulations are adopted.

I. Name and Organization

1. The name of this Association is and shall be The Northampton Association of Education and Industry.

2. The affairs of this Association shall be conducted by two bodies, viz. a Stock Company and an Industrial Community.

3. The Stock Company and the Industrial Community shall be distinct from each other in their organization, in their deliberations, and in their accounts, but the members of each body, shall be allowed to inspect the records and accounts both of the Industrial Community and of the Stock Company; and the Stock Directors may attend the meetings of the Industrial Directors and give their advice but shall not be allowed to vote, and the Industrial Directors may attend the meetings of the Stock Directors and give their advice but shall not be allowed to vote.

4. The association shall be organized by those persons who have paid three-fifths of the

amount of stock for which they have subscribed, and they shall choose from their own number a President, Treasurer, and Secretary. Those officers shall be *ex officio* Trustees of all the property of the Association, and members of the board of Stock Directors and of the Board of Industrial Directors. They shall be chosen annually by a majority of two-thirds of the votes of actual members; every officer of the Stock Company and of the Industrial Company shall be chosen annually by a like majority of each body respectively; and in all cases the voting shall be by ballot.

5. Every officer of the Association or of either of its departments shall at all times be removable by a majority of two-thirds of the votes of the body appointing him; and on the death, resignation, or removal of any trustee or other officer, he or his legal representative or representatives shall, on being suitably indemnified, be bound to convey to his successor in office at the expense of the Association all his property which had been previously held by or vested in him.

6. The President, Treasurer, and Secretary, with four additional members chosen from the Industrial Community, shall constitute a Board for the admission of new members, by a unanimous vote; and two-thirds of the votes of members of the Association at a regular meeting shall be requisite to the expulsion of a member, the decision to be confirmed by a similar majority at the next regular meeting.

7. Any member of the Association expelled or choosing to withdraw shall receive all that is his due at the next annual settlement, provided that he give ninety days previous notice and before receiving the balance due to him sign a full discharge of all claims against the Association, both as a Stock Company and an Industrial Community.

The Northampton Association of Education and Industry was organized on the 8th day of April, 1842, by the adoption of the preceding preamble, principles, and regulations, and by the appointment of Joseph Conant, S. L. Hill, and W. Adam, as *President, Treasurer,* and *Secretary* respectively, and as joint Trustees of the Association. The Trustees, on behalf of the Association, have purchased an Estate consisting of about four hundred and seventy acres of land, about seventy of which are covered with wood and timber; six frame dwelling-houses; a brick factory, nearly new, four stories high, measuring 120 by 40 feet, with water-wheel, gear, and shafting fit for operation, and situated on a durable stream of water having from 27 to 29 feet fall; a dye-house with necessary appartus; a frame building about 30 feet square, adapted for mechanical purposes, with water-wheel and other fixtures; a saw-mill; a Raymond's shingle-mill, capable of cutting 10,000 shingles per hour, with patent right secured for the town of Northampton; a planing machine for planing and jointing boards, planks, and timber; turning lathes, circular saws, &c., &c., together with machinery in the factory adapted to the manufacture of silk, about 100,000 feet of pine lumber in logs and boards, about 250 cords of wood cut and corded, and sundry other articles of personal property.

It is requested that all communications on business connected with the Association may be addressed to the Secretary, William Adam, Northampton, Massachusetts.

The following Preamble and Articles of Association were adopted by the Northampton Association of Education and Industry, at the annual meeting, held agreeably to notice, on the 18th of January, 1843, as a modification for the present year, of the former Constitution.

The subscribers, members of the Northampton Association of Education and Industry, desirous of a better development of the true principles of association than is practicable under existing arrangements; believing at the present time when conviction is spreading over the world of the falsity and corruption of social institutions and when earnest and truthful minds are ready every where for a higher state, that it is especially necessary for all who raise the banner of reform and separate from existing evils, to assert and maintain clearly and energetically, in their fullest extent and purity, the principles of equal brotherhood, the all-embracing law of love so emphatically taught by true Christianity and destined to bestow upon social organization a beauty and truthfulness it has never before known; believing that this principle and this law recognize no distinction of rights and rewards between the strong and the weak, the skilful and the unskilful, the man and the woman, the rich and the poor, asking only of all honest effort according to ability; that they never accord to property peculiar privileges, but seek only to bring mankind into harmony and union, to make the earth with its countless products the common equal heritge of the race as *one great family*, and to prepare this family by an enlightened and never-ending education to be peaceful, happy and active fellow-laborers together; never permitting strength to monopolize or skill to appropriate selfishly, but welcoming all to an equal participation of God's blessed bounty.

Believing further that although after equal division of all the products of labor and of the soil, it is just and convenient that such equal division should beunder individual control as property, thereby to furnish liberty for individual management, taste, appropriation and economy, yet nevertheless, by the principles of true association, all capital whatever contributed by individuals to stock should come under the exclusive management of the body thus associating, subject to no other interference, and all having an equal voice in its regulation as *partners* fully united by one common enterprise, and recognizing no individual right in such contribution excepting that of the contributor to repayment upon withdrawal.

Finally, believing that in our united plan of life it should be our especial aim to appeal to and rely upon the highest principles of our nature, and to avoid the fostering of that spirit of selfish accumulation which cannot but be stimulated by the register and payment of each particular hour of service; and also that we should in no case delegate to any board or officer duties and responsibilities the constant exercise of which belongs properly to ourselves and is necessary for our own self education and maintenance of a watchful interest on the part of all, and believing that the power of receiving new members into our Association, and an equal voice in the management of its funds, are especially necessary in this respect: — Therefore, we do adopt for the better realization of the principles herein expressed and for our mutual convenience and regulation the following rules, suspending the operation for the present year of eighteen hundred and forty-three, of whatever articles of the Constitution may conflict with them.

1. All matters pertaining to the Stock of the Association, the appropriation or disposition of funds or sale and purchase of property, real and personal, shall be considered as within the control and management of the whole Association, in which all adult members are equally interested and shall have the same vote as they now have in other business of the Community

2. The Industrial Directors of all the Departments shall be chosen by ballot by the Community at large in public meeting, the Director of each particular Department being selected from the persons belonging to that Department, and the formation of new Departments shall also be in the power solely of the whole Association.

3. The members and families of members of the Association shall receive food, lodging, necessary furniture, fuel, oil, and clothing, in addition to what is provided by article 29th of the Constitution, at the common expense, which in order that they may be equally shared by all shall be provided in the following way. The Industrial Directors shall provide suitable tenements or rooms and necessary furniture for every individual or family, none being dispossessed of rooms or tenements once assigned to them without their consent and those furnishing their own rooms being credited with a fair rent for its use. Provisions and other articles shall be supplied from the Store Department to the boarding house and to all members and their families at cost and be charged when delivered, and fuel shall also be supplied by the Lumber Department in proper state for use. To meet all charges for subsistence and clothing, every member shall be credited with whatever shall be ascertained to be the actual expense of board, including fuel and light, at the Community boarding house for each individual, and the Industrial Directors shall also fix upon a suitable equal allowance for clothing to be credited alike to all members over the age of eighteen without distinction, and also a suitable allowance for members and children under that age, being equal to those of same age, a proper deduction being made by them from all allowances credited, for all absence not on Community business.

4. In the annual settlement of the accounts of the Association, after paying first for the subsistence of members and all necessary expenses, interest due on all borrowed capital shall be paid, also six per cent interest on all stock paid in by members of the Association. After these payments, the remaining net profits shall be divided equally among every adult member of the Association over the age of eighteen years, suitable deductions being made by the Industrial Board in all cases of absence not on Community business, and it being provided that three-fourths of the profits thus divided shall be invested by each member in the Stock of the Association and not be withdrawn until after four years from the time of its investment.

5. The power of admitting new members shall be with the Industrial Community alone, all applications for admission to be reported by the Secretary or any officer of the Association at the next succeeding regular business meeting of Industrial members, with whatever information may be had concerning such application, which shall then be submitted to the two following weekly business meetings and be finally acted upon at the last, the affirmative vote of two-thirds of the members voting being requisite for admission; — provided that the second of the three business meetings above referred to may by a unanimous vote dispense with any further delay and act upon the subject of admission at once.

6. The right of voting on all business of the Association shall be restricted to those over the age of eighteen years.

7. Trusting only to that law of love and brotherhood which should be our bond of union to stimulate all to a cheerful and hearty co-operation, we do agree most cordially and heartily to labor to the best of our ability for the common benefit of our Community, devoting when not prevented by necessary family and other duties at least sixty hours each week to active employment in the Departments where our services will be most advantageous, and striving always to promote our mutual advancement in good fellowship, knowledge and goodness.

8. It shall be the duty of the Secretary to call the annual meeting of the Association by giving ten days previous written notice of the time and place thereof to all the members, the meeting to be held on any day in the month of January and in any convenient building within the limits of the property of the Association; and meetings at which special business may be transacted shall be called in the same manner on the requisition of any five members of the Association addressed to the Secretary, the requisition in every instance to state the special business for which the meeting is to be convened.

9. The Trustees, with the concurrence of the Stock Directors, shall have the right to sell and convey in fee simple, or for other less estate any or all of the real personal property which is or may be in their hands on such terms as they shall think proper, without any obligation on the part of the purchaser to see to the application of the purchase-money, and thereupon they shall, as may be voted by the Stock Directors, either re-invest the proceeds of such sale, or employ them in carrying on or extending the industrial pursuits of the Community, or after discharging all claims against the Association divide the proceeds or any part thereof among the Stockholders in proportion to the amount of Stock which they have respectively paid in.

II. Stock Company

10. The Board of Directors of the Stock Company shall consist of the President, Treasurer, and Secretary of the Association, and of four additional members.

11. The Stock shall be in shares of $100 each; the Stock subscription shall be open until the subscriptions shall amount to $100,000; and those subscribers only who have paid three-fifths of their subscriptions shall be entitled to vote.

12. Stock may be paid in money or some equivalent, at the option of the Stock Directors; and if a person without any capital shall be deemed eligible as a member of the Association, and shall be desirous of subscribing Stock, he shall be permitted to subscribe for one or more shares to be paid from the proceeds of his labour; but he shall not be entitled to vote as a Stockholder or to receive interest or dividends on the sum at his credit, until it shall amount to three-fifths of the stock which stands in his name.

13. The Secretary shall keep a Register of the number of shares subscribed, the names of the shareholders, the amount of Stock paid, and interest and dividends due thereon. The Stock shall be negotiable, but no transfer thereof shall be valid unless endorsed by the President and Secretary and recorded on the Secretary's books. No transfer shall be authorized for any person indebted to the Association until security be given for the payment of his debt.

14. Stock shall be entitled to annual interest not exceeding six per cent; but interest shall not be payable under four years, when the simple interest for the four years then due may be paid, or the arrears may be equally divided between the next four years, at the option of the Stock Directors.

15. New Stock may be raised at any time and to any amount, determined by two-thirds of the votes of the Stockholders.

16. Children above the age of five years may hold Stock in their own names and may be

present at the meetings of Stockholders, but they shall not vote until they have attained the full age of sixteen years.

17. Interest or dividends of profits may be paid in Stock or cash, at the option of the Stockholder; but the Company shall not be obliged to pay cash, unless notice be given to the ☆ Secretary thirty days before the payment becomes due.

18. In Stock transactions every share shall be entitled to one vote provided that no shareholder shall be entitled to more than ten votes. In the absence of Stockholders their shares may be represented by proxies.

19. Those Stockholders who shall fail to pay such equal assessments, not exceeding one hundred dollars per share on the whole, as the Stock Directors may impose, shall cease to be entitled to vote as Stockholders or to receive interest or dividends on their Stock until the interest and dividends that would otherwise be payable to them shall amount to the assessment or assessments in arrear with interest at six per centum per annum.

20. Every certificate of Stock shall be held subject to the condition that shares owned by persons not members of the Industrial Community may be bought in upon payment of principal and interest, by members of the Community, provided that notice of such intention shall be given thirty days before the annual interest becomes due.

21. The President and Secretary shall sign all contracts and papers binding the Company, and the Treasurer shall give security to the satisfaction of the Company for the safe keeping of its money and papers.

22. The Secretary shall keep account of all the property, contracts and obligations of the Company, and of the obligations and money-transactions of each member with the Company.

23. The Secretary shall make annually an inventory of all the property of the Association, an adjusted statement of its pecuniary condition, and a full settlement of its transactions with each member of the Company and with other parties, so that at the begining of each year new accounts may be opened.

24. The Stock Directors will determine in what manner the funds of the Company shall be invested and will make such appropriations for carrying on the different branches of business, as they may judge best; those branches being most favored that are necessary and less attractive. After the actual payments of Stock shall amount to $31,200, they shall not possess the power, as officers and agents of the Company, to buy or sell on credit.

III. Industrial Community

25. The Industrial Community shall be organized by individual members and families uniting to constitute it; by establishing distinct departments of industry; and by electing a Director of each department.

26. Every member of the Industrial Community may devote himself to different departments of industry; and all the members belonging to any one department shall choose amongst themselves the Director of that department.

27. The Industrial Directors, with the President, Treasurer, and Secretary of the Association, shall form a Board who shall provide suitable employment for all the members, shall fix the rate of compensation for the various employments, awarding the highest compensation to the most necessary and disagreeable, and shall manage the purchase of materials and goods and the sale of articles produced or manufactured, but after the actual payments of Stock shall amount to $31,200, they shall have no power, as officers and agents of the Community, to buy or sell on credit.

28. Children above the age of five years may become members and be present at the meetings of members, and may engage in the industrial pursuits of the Community and receive compensation for their labour; but they shall not vote until they have attained the full age of sixteen years.

29. The Association shall provide for the members of the Industrial Community and their families, moral, literary, scientific, agricultural and mechanical instruction, medical attendance and nursing, baths and public rooms without charge; but every member shall be at liberty to seek and procure for himself and his family other instruction, medical attendance, and nursing, at his own cost.

30. If labour in kind or in quantity is required which the Industrial Community does not supply, it may be hired for the occasion at the expense of the Association; if the Industrial Directors cannot furnish constant labor to be for the benefit of the Association; and if any members shall prefer employment not under the direction of the Industrial Community, they may engage in it, with the consent of the Directors, for the benefit of the Association.

31. Every man, woman and child above the age of five years, being members, shall have a separate account with the Association.

32. Every member of the Industrial Community shall live on the lands belonging to the Association and shall be provided with suitable apartments; and in settling with individual members each shall be credited with the value of labour performed, and charged at a reasonable rate with the rent of apartments occupied and at cost with articles for domestic consumption.

33. In making the annual settlement, the disbursements shall be made in the following order; 1st, the wages of labour; 2nd, the expense of supporting members of the Industrial Community unable to earn a livelihood by their own labour, including destitute widows and orphans of deceased members, the property of such members in the Stock account being first applied as far as it will go; 3rd, interest on Stock; and 4th, the net balance, if any, shall be divided among the members of the Association, one half being awarded to labour, one-fourth to skill, and one-fourth to capital.

34. Any matter in dispute shall be decided by arbitration. The two parties concerned shall each select an arbitrator. The two arbitrators thus selected shall choose a third. And the three thus chosen shall constitute a Board of arbitration who shall in open court hear the representations and examine the witnesses of both parties and shall deliver a written decision, conformable to equity and good conscience, which shall be binding without appeal and shall be placed on record for future reference and guidance. The arbitrators shall be compensated for their time and labour by the Association according to a rate fixed by the Industrial Directors.

35. The litigation in a court of law of any question in dispute between parties belonging to the Association, either instead of having recourse to arbitration or for the purpose of overthrowing a decision pronounced by arbitrators, shall subject the offender to expulsion.

36. The Association may establish By-laws not inconsistent with the spirit and intention of this Constitution.

37. The provisions of this Constitution may be altered by a majority of two-thirds of the votes of the members, provided notice of the proposed alteration shall be given in the manner to be prescribed in the By-laws.

APPENDIX C

MEMBERSHIP LIST*

The system adopted by the association of admitting members on probation accounts for the apparent errors in the list below, which is copied from the book kept by the secretary. People often resided in the community for a year before being admitted as regular members. During the last twelve months the secretary did not take very great pains to enter names and withdrawals, and in some cases these have been supplied from the reports.

Names	From	Entered	Withdrew
William Adams, wife, 4 children	Cambridge	April 18, 1842	Jan. 2, 1844
James D. Atkins	Old Cambridge	Sept. 28, 1842	Mar. 6, 1847
George Ashley	Chaplin, Ct.	Jan. 13, 1844	Dec. 28, 1845
George Benson, wife, 4 children	Brooklyn, Ct.	April 8, 1842	Oct. 1, 1845
Frances P. Birge[1]	Colebrook, Ct.	May 28, 1842	
Samuel Brooks, wife, 7 children	Hadley	April 9, 1842	March 1843
Samuel A. Bottum, wife	Mansfield, Ct.	April 8, 1842	Oct. 13, 1843
Roxey A. Brown[2]	Bloomfield, Ct.	Nov. 12, 1842	
James Boyle, wife	Boston	June 5, 1842	
Wm. J. Bumstead, wife, 3 children	Bloomfield, Ct.	Nov. 16, 1842	
Luther Brigham, 4 children	Worcester	Nov. 29, 1843	
Susan Byrne	Willimantic, Ct.	Nov. 4, 1843	July 1844
William Bassett, wife, 4 children	Lynn	Feb. 24, 1844	Nov. 18, 1844
Cyrus Bradbury	Boston	April 4, 1844	Dec. 2, 1844
Elizabeth Ely Bradbury	Boston	April 4, 1844	
Sarah Elizabeth Bradbury	Boston	April 4, 1844	
Bailey Birge, wife, 3 children	Colebrook, Ct.	Jan. 31, 1846	
Joseph Conant, wife	Mansfield, Ct.	April 8, 1842	Oct. 8, 1842
Orwell S. Chaffee, wife, 1 child	Mansfield, Ct.	April 24, 1842	Oct. 22, 1842
George Cooper	Mansfield, Ct.	April 15, 1843	Sept. 12, 1843
Octavia M. Damon[3]	Chesterfield	Sept. 30, 1844	March 6, 1847
Sophia Foorde	Dedham	April 15, 1843	June 12, 1845
Emily Farwell	Cambridge	June 17, 1843	
Gustavus Gifford	Nantucket	Nov. 29, 1842	
Roswell K. Goodwin		Nov. 25, 1843	
Caroline M. Gove	Lynn	June 25, 1844	
Erasmus G. Hudson, wife, 2 children	Bloomfield, Ct.	April 8, 1842	Sept. 16, 1843
Rhoda Hudson	Wolcottville	Feb. 11, 1843	May 13, 1843
Romulus Fowler Hudson	Bloomfield, Ct.	April 8, 1842	
Samuel L. Hill, wife, 3 children	Willimantic, Ct.	April 8, 1842	
Sally Hill, 4 children	Northampton	April 8, 1842	Sept. 23, 1842
Josiah Hayward, wife, 3 children	Salem	March 8, 1843	July 2, 1844
William Haven, wife, 7 children	Windham, Ct.	May 4, 1843	
Matilda Hill, 4 children	Willimantic, Ct.	Jan. 13, 1844	

---

*Reprinted from Charles A. Sheffeld, ed., *The History of Florence, Massachusetts* (Florence, Mass.: published by the editor, 1895), pp. 103-105.

[1]Married Hall Judd, June 1, 1842
[2]Married A. R. Nickerson, June 8, 1844
[3]Married James D. Atkins, Sept. 30, 1844

Harriet W. Hayden[4]	Bath, Me.	April 10, 1844	
Lucy Charlotte Hayden	Bath, Me.	April 10, 1844	
Elisha L. Hammond, wife	New Ipswich, N.H.	May 16, 1844	Nov. 1, 1846
Hall Judd	Northampton	May 28, 1842	
William Larned	Boston	Oct. 15, 1842	Aug. 2, 1843
David Mack, wife, 2 children	Cambridge	May 15, 1842	Sept. 5, 1845
Charles May	Benton, Ala.	Jan. 13, 1843	
Abner S. Meade	Danvers	Dec. 6, 1842	
Littleton T. Morgan	Cambridge	July 28, 1842	
Moses K. Meader	Nantucket	April 15, 1843	April 3, 1844
George W. Miller	Boston	July 22, 1843	
A. Menkin, M.D.		Jan. 13, 1844	March 1844
Joseph C. Martin, wife, 4 children	Chaplin, Ct.	April 9, 1844	
Lorenzo D. Nickerson	Boston	April 15, 1843	Nov. 1843
Enos L. Preston, wife, 1 child	Brooklyn, Ct.	Sept. 3, 1842	July 1843
William F. Parker, wife, 2 children	Nantucket	Oct. 22, 1842	
Susan F. Parker	Nantucket	Jan. 14, 1843	
Oliver D. Paine	Chesterfield	April 10, 1842	June 16, 1845
George Prindle	New Haven, Ct.	May 13, 1843	May 1845
Fortune R. Porter	New York	Aug. 19, 1843	Jan. 31, 1844
Lydia B. Pierce		Feb. 25, 1843	
Nancy Richardson, 4 children	Waltham	Sept. 24, 1842	
David Ruggles	New York	Nov. 30, 1842	
Stephen C. Rush	New York	Nov.4, 1843	April 23, 1846
Lucius F. Reede	Cummington	May 20, 1843	Nov. 1843
Austin Ross, wife	Chaplin, Ct.	Mar. 29, 1845	
Ezra Rosbrooks	Cicero, N.Y.	Jan. 26, 1844	
Polly Rosbrooks	Cicero, N.Y.	Jan. 26, 1844	
Louisa C. Rosbrooks	Cicero, N.Y.	Jan. 26, 1844	
Francis O. Rosbrooks	Cicero, N.Y.	Jan. 26, 1844	
Three Rosbrooks children	Cicero, N.Y.	Jan. 26, 1844	
Theodore Scarborough, wife, 1 child	Brooklyn, Ct.	April 8, 1842	
Jason Sullaway, wife	Canton	April 17, 1842	
Pamelia Small, 1 child	Norwich, Ct.	April 8, 1842	May 31, 1845
Earle Dwight Swift, wife	Mansfield, Ct.	April 8, 1842	Oct. 1842
Herbert Scarborough	Brooklyn, Ct.	Jan. 14, 1843	
Mary Ann Smith	Bloomfield, Ct.	Jan. 8, 1843	

---

[4]Married Sidney Southworth, July 3, 1844

ABOUT THE AUTHOR

Alice Eaton McBee, 2nd, received her A.B. from Sweet Briar College in 1941 and a B.S. in Library Service from Columbia University in 1943. The following two years were spent as librarian at the Hillyer Art Gallery at Smith College. In 1945 she was awarded a teaching-fellowship in the History Department and received her M.A. from Smith in 1946. She is now teaching history at the Northampton School for Girls.

STATEMENT OF PURPOSE

The *Smith College Studies in History* have completed (by the end of 1945) thirty years of continuous publication. During that period they have published 55 books and monographs. Twenty-one of them concerned American general, social and cultural history; ten, the social and economic development of the Connecticut Valley; four, United States foreign relations and diplomatic history; seven, English history (mediaeval and modern); and eleven, European history (1 ancient, 2 mediaeval, 5 Renaissance and early modern period, 3 Europe since the French Revolution). Of the two remaining *Studies* one, by Harold J. Laski, dealt with "The problem of administration areas," and the other with the history of the Smith College department of history and government from 1875 to 1920.

Special emphasis was given to "regional" history. The first volume of the *Studies* was an "Introduction to the history of Connecticut as a manufacturing State," and during the last years the results of the research of the Smith College Council of Industrial Studies have been published in the *Studies*. But from the beginning the *Studies* intended to cover as wide a field in historical scholarship as possible. The second year of publication started with Sidney B. Fay's "The Hohenzollern household and administration in the sixteenth century," and before long, monographs as varied as William D. Gray's "Study of the life of Hadrian prior to his accession" and Elizabeth A. Foster's "Le Dernier Séjour de J. J. Rousseau à Paris 1770–1778" appeared under the imprint of the *Smith College Studies*. As to the fields covered, the following *Studies* may give a sufficient suggestion: Marcus Hansen, "German schemes of colonization before 1860"; J. Fred Rippy, "The historical background of the American policy of isolation"; Merle Curti, "Bryan and world peace"; Eunice M. Shuster, "Native American anarchism"; Sidney R. Packard, "Records of the Norman exchequer, 1199–1204"; Vera L. Brown, "Studies in the history of Spain in the second half of the 18th century"; Florence A. Gragg and Leona C. Gabel, "The Commentaries of Pius II"; L. S. Stavrianos, "Balkan Federation."